How to Observe Morals and Manners

By Harriet Martineau

Table of contents

Hélas! où donc chercher, où trouver le bonheur?
----Nulle part tout entier, partout avec mesure.

Voltaire

Opening my journal-book, and dipping my pen in my ink-horn, I
determined, as far as I could, to justify myself and my
countrymen in wandering over the face of the earth.

Rogers

Preface

"The best mode of exciting the love of observation is by teaching 'How to Observe.' With this end it was originally intended to produce, in one or two volumes, a series of hints for travellers and students, calling their attention to the points necessary for inquiry or observation in the different branches of Geology, Natural History, Agriculture, the Fine Arts, General Statistics, and Social Manners. On consideration, however, it was determined somewhat to extend the plan, and to separate the great divisions of the field of observation, so that those whose tastes led them to one particular branch of inquiry might not be encumbered with other parts in which they do not feel an equal interest."

The preceding passage is contained in the notice accompanying the first work in this series--Geology, by Mr. De la Bèche, published in 1835. Thus, the second work in the series is in continuation of the plan above announced.

Part One: Requisites for Observation

Introduction

Inest sua gratia parvis.
Les petites choses n'ont de valeur que de la part de ceux qui
peuvent s'élever aux grandes.

--De Jouy.

There is no department of inquiry in which it is not full as easy to miss truth as to find it, even when the materials from which truth is to be drawn are actually present to our senses. A child does not catch a gold fish in water at the first trial, however good his eyes may be, and however clear the water; knowledge and method are necessary to enable him to take what is actually before his eyes and under his hand. So it is with all who fish in a strange element for the truth which is living and moving there: the powers of observation must be trained, and habits of method in arranging the materials presented to the eye must be acquired before the student possesses the requisites for understanding what he contemplates.

The observer of Men and Manners stands as much in need of intellectual preparation as any other student. This is not, indeed, generally supposed, and a multitude of travellers act as if it were not true. Of the large number of tourists who annually sail from our ports, there is probably not one who would dream of pretending to make observations on any subject of physical inquiry, of which he did not understand even the principles. If, on his return from the Mediterranean, the unprepared traveller was questioned about the geology of Corsica, or the public buildings of Palermo, he would reply, "Oh, I can tell you nothing about that--I never studied geology; I know nothing about architecture." But few, or none, make the same avowal about the morals and manners of a nation. Every man seems to imagine that he can understand men at a glance; he supposes that it is enough to be among them to know what they are doing; he thinks that eyes, ears, and memory are enough for morals, though they would not qualify him for botanical or statistical observation; he pronounces confidently upon the merits and social condition of the nations among whom he has travelled; no misgiving ever prompts him to say, "I can give you little general information about the people I have been seeing; I have not studied the principles of morals; I am no judge of national manners."

There would be nothing to be ashamed of in such an avowal. No wise man blushes at being ignorant of any science which it has not suited his purposes to study, or which it has not been in his power to attain. No linguist wrings his hands when astronomical discoveries are talked of in his presence; no political economist covers his face when shown a shell or a plant which he cannot class; still less should the artist, the natural philosopher, the commercial traveller, or the classical scholar, be ashamed to own himself unacquainted with the science which, of all the sciences which have yet opened upon men, is, perhaps, the least cultivated, the least definite, the least ascertained in itself, and the most difficult in its application.

In this last characteristic of the science of Morals lies the excuse of as many travellers as may decline pronouncing on the social condition of any people. Even if the generality of travellers were as enlightened as they are at present ignorant about the principles of Morals, the difficulty of putting those principles to interpretative uses would deter the wise from making the hasty decisions, and uttering the large judgments, in which travellers have hitherto been wont to indulge. In proportion as men become sensible how infinite are the diversities in man, how incalculable the varieties and influences of circumstances, rashness of pretension and decision will abate, and the great work of classifying the moral manifestations of society will be confided to the philosophers, who bear the same relation to the science of society as Herschel does to astronomy, and Beaufort to hydrography.

Of all the tourists who utter their decisions upon foreigners, how many have begun their researches at home? Which of them would venture upon giving an account of the morals and manners of London, though he may have lived in it all his life? Would any one of them escape errors as gross as those of the Frenchman who published it as a general fact that people in London always have, at dinner parties, soup on each side, and fish at four corners? Which of us would undertake to classify the morals and manners of any hamlet in England, after spending the summer in it? What sensible man seriously generalizes upon the manners of a street, even though it be Houndsditch or Cranbourn-Alley? Who pretends to explain all the proceedings of his next-door neighbor? Who is able to account for all that is said and done by the dweller in the same house,--by parent, child, brother, or domestic? If such judgments were attempted, would they not be as various as those who make them? And would they not, after all, if closely looked into, reveal more of the mind of the observer than of the observed?

If it be thus with us at home, amidst all the general resemblances, the prevalent influences which furnish an interpretation to a large number of facts, what hope of a trustworthy judgment remains for the foreign tourist, however good may be his method of travelling, and however long his absence from home? He looks at all the people along his line of road, and converses with a few individuals from among them. If he diverges, from time to time, from the high road,--if he winds about among villages, and crosses mountains, to dip into the hamlets of the valleys,--he still pursues only a line, and does not command the expanse; he is furnished, at best, with no more than a sample of the people; and whether they be indeed a sample, must remain a conjecture which he has no means of verifying. He converses, more or less, with, perhaps, one man in ten thousand of those he sees; and of the few with whom he converses, no two are alike in powers and in training, or perfectly agree in their views on any one of the great subjects which the traveller professes to observe; the information afforded by one is contradicted by another; the fact of one day is proved error by the next; the wearied mind soon finds itself overwhelmed by the multitude of unconnected or contradictory particulars, and lies passive to be run over by the crowd. The tourist is no more likely to learn, in this way, the social state of a nation, than his valet would be qualified to speak of the meteorology of the country from the number of times the umbrellas were wanted in the course of two months. His children might as well undertake to exhibit the geological formation of the country from the pebbles they picked up in a day's ride.

I remember some striking words addressed to me, before I set out on my travels, by a wise man, since dead. "You are going to spend two years in the United States," said he. "Now just tell me,--do you expect to understand the Americans by the time you come back? You do not: that is well. I lived five-and-twenty years in Scotland, and I fancied I understood the Scotch; then I came to England, and supposed I should soon understand the English. I have now lived five-and-twenty years here, and I begin to think I understand neither the Scotch nor the English."

What is to be done? Let us first settle what is not to be done.

The traveller must deny himself all indulgence of peremptory decision, not only in public on his return, but in his journal, and in his most superficial thoughts. The experienced and conscientious traveller would word the condition differently. Finding peremptory decision more trying to his conscience than agreeable to his laziness, he would call it not indulgence, but anxiety; he enjoys the employment of collecting materials, but would shrink from the responsibility of judging a community.

The traveller must not generalize on the spot, however true may be his apprehension--however firm his grasp, of one or more facts. A raw English traveller in China was entertained by a host who was intoxicated, and a hostess who was red-haired; he immediately made a note of the fact that all the men in China were drunkards, and all the women red-haired. A raw Chinese traveller in England was landed by a Thames waterman who had a wooden leg. The stranger saw that the wooden leg was used to stand in the water with, while the other was high and dry. The apparent economy of the fact struck the Chinese; he saw in it strong evidence of design, and wrote home that in England one-legged men are kept for watermen, to the saving of all injury to health, shoe, and stocking, from standing in the river. These anecdotes exhibit but a slight exaggeration of the generalizing tendencies of many modern travellers. They are not so much worse than some recent tourists' tales, as they are better than the old narratives of "men whose heads do grow beneath their shoulders."

Natural philosophers do not dream of generalizing with any such speed as that used by the observers of men; yet they might do it with more safety, at the risk of an incalculably smaller mischief. The geologist and the chemist make a large collection of particular appearances, before they commit themselves to propound a principle drawn from them, though their subject matter is far less diversified than the human subject, and nothing of so much importance as human emotions,--love and dislike, reverence and contempt, depends upon their judgment. If a student in natural philosophy is in too great haste to classify and interpret, he misleads, for a while, his fellow-students (not a very large class); he vitiates the observations of a few successors; his error is discovered and exposed; he is mortified, and his too docile followers are ridiculed, and there is an end; but if a traveller gives any quality which he may have observed in a few individuals as a characteristic of a nation, the evil is not speedily or easily remediable. Abject thinkers, passive readers, adopt his words; parents repeat them to their children; and townspeople spread the judgment into the villages and hamlets--the strongholds of prejudice; future travellers see according to the prepossessions given them, and add their testimony to the error, till it becomes the work of a century to reverse a hasty generalization. It was a great mistake of a geologist to assign a wrong level to the Caspian Sea; and it is vexatious that much time and energy should have been devoted to account for an appearance which, after all, does not exist. It is provoking to geologists that they should have wasted a great deal of ingenuity in finding reasons for these waters being at a different level from what it is now found that they have; but the evil is over; the "pish!" and the "pshaw!" are said; the explanatory and apological notes are duly inserted in new editions of geological works, and nothing more can come of the mistake. But it is difficult to foresee when the British public will believe that the Americans are a mirthful nation, or even that the French are not almost all cooks or dancing-masters. A century hence, probably, the Americans will continue to believe that all the English make a regular study of the art of conversation; and the lower orders of French will be still telling their children that half the people in England hang or drown themselves every November. As long as travellers generalize on morals and manners as hastily as they do, it will probably be impossible to establish a general conviction that no civilized nation is ascertainably better or worse than any other on this side barbarism, the whole field of morals being taken into the view. As long as travellers continue to neglect the safe means of generalization which are within the reach of all, and build theories upon the manifestations of individual minds, there is little hope of inspiring men with that spirit of impartiality, mutual deference, and love, which are the best enlighteners of the eyes and rectifiers of the understanding.

Above all things, the traveller must not despair of good results from his observations. Because he cannot establish true conclusions by imperfect means, he is not to desist from doing anything at all. Because he cannot safely generalize in one way, it does not follow that there is no other way. There are methods of safe generalization of which I shall speak by-and-by. But, if there were not such within his reach, if his only materials were the discourse, the opinions, the feelings, the way of life, the looks, dress, and manners of individuals, he might still afford important contributions to science by his observations on as wide a variety of these as he can bring within his mental grasp. The experience of a large number of observers would in time yield materials from which a cautious philosopher might draw conclusions. It is a safe rule, in morals as in physics, that no fact is without its use. Every observer and recorder is fulfilling a function; and no one observer or recorder ought to feel discouragement, as long as he desires to be useful rather than shining; to be the servant rather than the lord of science, and a friend to the home-stayers rather than their dictator.

One of the wisest men living writes to me, "No books are so little to be trusted as travels. All travellers do and must generalize too rapidly. Most, if not all, take a fact for a principle, or the exception for the rule, more or less; and the quickest minds, which love to reason and explain more than to observe with patience, go most astray. My faith in travels received a mortal wound when I travelled. I read, as I went along, the books of those who had preceded me, and found that we did not see with the same eyes. Even descriptions of nature proved false. The traveller had viewed the prospect at a different season, or in a different light, and substituted the transient for the fixed. Still I think travels useful. Different accounts give means of approximation to truth; and by-and-by what is fixed and essential in a people will be brought out."

It ought to be an animating thought to a traveller that, even if it be not in his power to settle any one point respecting the morals and manners of an empire, he can infallibly aid in supplying means of approximation to truth, and of bringing out "what is fixed and essential in a people." This should be sufficient to stimulate his exertions and satisfy his ambition.

Chapter 1: Philosophical Requisites

Only I believe that this is not a bow for every man to shoot in
that counts himself a teacher, but will require sinews almost
equal to those which Homer gave Ulysses; yet I am withal
persuaded that it may prove much more easy in the essay than it
now seems at a distance.

--Milton

There are two parties to the work of observation on Morals and Manners--
the observer and the observed. This is an important fact which the traveller
seldom dwells upon as he ought; yet a moment's consideration shows that the
mind of the observer--the instrument by which the work is done, is as
essential as the material to be wrought. If the instrument be in bad order, it
will furnish a bad product, be the material what it may. In this chapter I shall
point out what requisites the traveller ought to make sure that he is possessed
of before he undertakes to offer observations on the Morals and Manners of a
people.

Section 1

He must have made up his mind as to what it is that he wants to know. In
physical science, great results may be obtained by hap-hazard experiments;
but this is not the case in Morals. A chemist can hardly fail of learning
something by putting any substances together, under new circumstances, and
seeing what will arise out of the combination; and some striking discoveries
happened in this way, in the infancy of the science; though no one doubts that
more knowledge may be gained by the chemist who has an aim in his mind,
and who conducts his experiment on some principle. In Morals, the latter
method is the only one which promises any useful results. In the workings of
the social system, all the agents are known in the gross--all are determined. It

is not their nature, but the proportions in which they are combined, which have to be ascertained.

What does the traveller want to know? He is aware that, wherever he goes, he will find men, women, and children; strong men and weak men; just men and selfish men. He knows that he will everywhere find a necessity for food, clothing, and shelter; and everywhere some mode of general agreement how to live together. He knows that he will everywhere find birth, marriage, and death; and therefore domestic affections. What results from all these elements of social life does he mean to look for?

For want of settling this question, one traveller sees nothing truly, because the state of things is not consistent with his speculations as to how human beings ought to live together; another views the whole with prejudice, because it is not like what he has been accustomed to see at home; yet each of these would shrink from the recognition of his folly, if it were fully placed before him. The first would be ashamed of having tried any existing community by an arbitrary standard of his own--an act much like going forth into the wilderness to see kings' houses full of men in soft raiment; and the other would perceive that different nations may go on judging one another by themselves till doomsday, without in any way improving the chance of self-advancement and mutual understanding. Going out with the disadvantage of a habit of mind uncounteracted by an intellectual aim, will never do. The traveller may as well stay at home, for anything he will gain in the way of social knowledge.

The two considerations just mentioned must be subordinated to the grand one,--the only general one,--of the relative amount of human happiness. Every element of social life derives its importance from this great consideration. The external conveniences of men, their internal emotions and affections, their social arrangements, graduate in importance precisely in proportion as they affect the general happiness of the section of the race among whom they exist. Here then is the wise traveller's aim,--to be kept in view to the exclusion of prejudice, both philosophical and national. He must not allow himself to be perplexed or disgusted by seeing the great ends of human association pursued by means which he could never have devised, and to the practice of which he could not reconcile himself. He is not to conclude unfavourably about the diet of the multitude because he sees them swallowing blubber, or scooping out watermelons, instead of regaling themselves with beef and beer. He is not to suppose their social meetings a failure because they eat with their fingers instead of with silver forks, or touch foreheads instead of making a bow. He is not to conclude against domestic morals, on account of a diversity of methods of entering upon marriage. He might as well judge of the minute transactions of manners all over the world by what he sees in his native village. There, to leave the door open or to shut it bears no relation to morals, and but little to manners; whereas, to shut the door is as cruel an act in a Hindoo hut as to leave it open in a Greenland cabin. In short, he is to prepare himself to bring whatever he may observe to the test of some high and broad principle, and not to that of a low comparative practice. To test one people by another, is to argue within a very small segment of a circle; and the observer can only pass backwards and forwards at an equal distance from the point of truth. To test the morals and manners of a nation by a reference to the essentials of human happiness, is to strike at once to the center, and to see things as they are.

Section 2

Being provided with a conviction of what it is that he wants to know, the traveller must be furthermore furnished with the means of gaining the knowledge he wants. When he was a child, he was probably taught that eyes, ears, and understanding are all-sufficient to gain for him as much knowledge as he will have time to acquire; but his self-education has been a poor one, if he has not become convinced that something more is needful--the enlightenment and discipline of the understanding, as well as its immediate use. It is not enough for a traveller to have an active understanding, equal to an accurate perception of individual facts in themselves; he must also be in possession of principles which may serve as a rallying point for his observations, and without which he cannot determine their bearings, or be secure of putting a right interpretation upon them. A traveller may do better without eyes, or without ears, than without such principles, as there is evidence to prove. Holman, the blind traveller, gains a wonderful amount of information, though he is shut out from the evidence yielded by the human countenance, by way-side groups, by the aspect of cities, and the varying phenomena of country regions. In his motto, he indicates something of his method.

> Sightless to see, and judge thro' judgment's eyes,
> To make four senses do the work of five,
> To arm the mind for hopeful enterprise,
> Are lights to him who doth in darkness live.

In order to "judge through judgment's eyes," those eyes must be made strong and clear; and a traveller may gain more without the bodily organ than with an untrained understanding. The case of the Deaf Traveller[A] leads us to say the same about the other great avenue of knowledge. His writings

15

prove, to all who are acquainted with them, that, though to a great degree deprived of that inestimable commentary upon perceived facts--human discourse--the Deaf Traveller is able to furnish us with more knowledge of foreign people than Fine-Ear himself could have done without the accompaniments of analytical power and concentrative thought. All senses, and intellectual powers, and good habits, may be considered essential to a perfect observation of morals and manners; but almost any one might be better spared than a provision of principles which may serve as a rallying point and a test of facts. The blind and the deaf travellers must suffer under a deprivation or deficiency of certain classes of facts. The condition of the unphilosophical traveller is much worse. It is a chance whether he puts a right interpretation on any of the facts he perceives.

Many may object that I am making much too serious a matter of the department of the business of travelling under present notice. They do not pretend to be moral philosophers;--they do not desire to be oracles;--they attempt nothing more than to give a simple report of what has come under their notice. But what work on earth is more serious than this of giving an account of the most grave and important things which are transacted on this globe? Every true report is a great good; every untrue report is a great mischief. Therefore, let there be none given but by persons in some good degree qualified. Such travellers as will not take pains to provide themselves with the requisite thought and study should abstain from reporting at all.

It is a mistake, however, to suppose that the study shown to be requisite is vast and deep. Some knowledge of the principles of Morals and the rule of Manners is required, as in the case of other sciences to be brought into use on a similar occasion; but the principles are few and simple, and the rule easy of application.

The universal summary notions of Morals may serve a common traveller in his judgments as to whether he would like to live in any foreign country, and as to whether the people there are as agreeable to him as his own nation. For such an one it may be sufficient to bear about the general notions that lying, thieving, idleness, and licentiousness are bad; and that truth, honesty, industry, and sobriety are good; and for common purposes, such an one may be trusted to pronounce what is industry and what idleness; what is licentiousness and what sobriety. But vague notions, home prepossessions, even on these great points of morals, are not sufficient, in the eyes of an enlightened traveller, to warrant decisions on the moral state of nations who are reared under a wide diversity of circumstances. The true liberality which alone is worthy to contemplate all the nations of the earth, does not draw a broad line through the midst of human conduct, declaring all that falls on the one side vice, and all on the other virtue; such a liberality knows that actions and habits do not always carry their moral impress visibly to all eyes, and that the character of very many must be determined by a cautious application of a few deep principles. Is the Shaker of New England a good judge of the morals and manners of the Arab of the Desert? What sort of a verdict would the shrewdest gipsy pass upon the monk of La Trappe? What would the Scotch peasant think of the magical practices of Egypt? or the Russian soldier of a meeting of electors in the United States? The ideas of right and wrong in the minds of these people are not of the enlarged kind which would enable them to judge persons in situations the most opposite to their own. The true philosopher, the worthy observer, first contemplates in imagination the area of humanity, and then ascertains what principles of morals are applicable to them all, and judges by these.

The enlightened traveller, if he explore only one country, carries in his mind the image of all; for, only in its relation to the whole of the race can anyone people be judged. Almost without exaggeration, he may be said to see what the rhapsodist in Volney saw.

"There, from above the atmosphere, looking down upon the earth I had quitted, I beheld a scene entirely new. Under my feet, floating in empty space, a globe similar to that of the moon, but less luminous, presented to me one of its faces.... 'What!' exclaimed I, 'is that the earth which is inhabited by human beings?'"[B]

The differences are, that, instead of "one of its faces," the moralist would see the whole of the earth in one contemplation; and that, instead of a nebulous expanse here, and a brown or grey speck there,--continents, seas, or volcanoes,--he would look into the homes and social assemblies of all lands. In the extreme North, there is the snow-hut of the Esquimaux, shining with the fire within, like an alabaster lamp left burning in a wide waste; within, the beardless father is mending his weapons made of fishbones, while the dwarfed mother swathes her infant in skins, and feeds it with oil and fat. In the extreme East, there is the Chinese family in their garden, treading its paved walks, or seated under the shade of its artificial rocks; the master displaying the claws of his left hand as he smokes his pipe, and his wife tottering on her deformed feet as she follows her child,--exulting over it if it be a boy; grave and full of sighs if heaven have sent her none but girls. In the extreme South, there is the Colonist of the Cape, lazily basking before his door, while he sends his laborer abroad with his bullock-wagon, devolves the business of the farm upon the women, and scares from his door any poor Hottentot who may have wandered hither over the plain. In the extreme West, there is the gathering together on the shores of the Pacific of the hunters laden with furs. The men are trading, or cleaning their arms, or sleeping; the squaws are cooking, or dyeing with vegetable juices the quills of the porcupine or the

17

hair of the moose-deer. In the intervals between these extremities, there is a world of morals and manners, as diverse as the surface of the lands on which they are exhibited. Here is the Russian nobleman on his estate, the lord of the fate of his serfs, but hard pressed by the enmity of rival nobles, and silenced by the despotism of his prince; his wife leads a languid life among her spinning maidens; and his young sons talk of the wars in which they shall serve their emperor in time to come. There is the Frankfort trader, dwelling among equals, fixing his pride upon having wronged no man, or upon having a son distinguished at the university, or a daughter skilled in domestic accomplishments; while his wife emulates her neighbors in supporting the comfort and respectability of the household. Here is the French peasant returning from the field in total ignorance of what has taken place in the capital of late; and there is the English artizan discussing with his brother-workman the politics of the town, or carrying home to his wife some fresh hopes of the interference of parliament about labor and wages. Here is a conclave of Cardinals, consulting upon the interests of the Holy See; there a company of Brahmins setting an offering of rice before their idol. In one direction, there is a handful of citizens building a new town in the midst of a forest; in another, there is a troop of horsemen hovering on the horizon, while a caravan is traversing the Desert. Under the twinkling shadows of a German vineyard, national songs are sung; from the steep places of the Swiss mountains the Alp-horn resounds; in the coffee-house at Cairo, listeners hang upon the voice of the romance reciter; the churches of Italy echo with solemn hymns; and the soft tones of the child are heard, in the New England parlor, as the young scholar reads the Bible to parent or aged grandfather.

All these, and more, will a traveller of the most enlightened order revolve before his mind's eye as he notes the groups which are presented to his senses. Of such travellers there are but too few; and vague and general, or merely traditional, notions of right and wrong must serve the purpose of the greater number. The chief evil of moral notions being vague or traditional is, that they are irreconcilable with liberality of judgment; and the great benefit of an ascertainment of the primary principles of morals is, that such an investigation dissolves prejudice, and casts a full light upon many things which cease to be fearful and painful when they are no longer obscure. We all know how different a Sunday in Paris appears to a sectarian, to whom the word of his priest is law; and to a philosopher, in whom religion is indigenous, who understands the narrowness of sects, and sees how much smaller even Christendom itself is than Humanity. We all know how offensive the prayers of Mahomedans at the corners of streets, and the pomp of catholic processions, are to those who know no other way than entering into their closet, and shutting the door when they pray; but how felt the deep thinker who wrote the Religio Medici? He was an orderly member of a Protestant church, yet he uncovered his head at the sight of a crucifix; he could not laugh at pilgrims walking with peas in their shoes, or despise a begging friar; he could "not hear an Ave Maria bell without an elevation;" and it is probable that even the Teraphim of the Arabs would not have been wholly absurd, or the car of Juggernaut itself altogether odious in his eyes. Such is the contrast between the sectary and the philosopher.

Section 3

As an instance of the advantage which a philosophical traveller has over an unprepared one, look at the difference which will enter into a man's judgment of nations, according as he carries about with him the vague popular notion of a Moral Sense, or has investigated the laws under which feelings of right and wrong grow up in all men. It is worthwhile to dwell a little on this important point.

Most persons who take no great pains to think for themselves, have a notion that every human being has feelings, or a conscience, born with him, by which he knows, if he will only attend to it, exactly what is right and wrong; and that, as right and wrong are fixed and immutable, all ought to agree as to what is sin and virtue in every case. Now, mankind are, and always have been, so far from agreeing as to right and wrong, that it is necessary to account in some manner for the wide differences in various ages, and among various nations. A great diversity of doctrines has been put forth for the purpose of lessening the difficulty; but they all leave certain portions of the race under the condemnation or compassion of the rest for their error, blindness, or sin. Moreover, no doctrines yet invented have accounted for some total revolutions in the ideas of right and wrong, which have occurred in the course of ages. A person who takes for granted that there is an universal Moral Sense among men, as unchanging as he who bestowed it, cannot reasonably explain how it was that those men were once esteemed the most virtuous who killed the most enemies in battle, while now it is considered far more noble to save life than to destroy it. They cannot but wonder how it was that it was once thought a great shame to live in misery, and an honor to commit suicide; while now the wisest and best men think exactly the reverse. And, with regard to the present age, it must puzzle men who suppose that all ought to think alike on moral subjects, that there are parts of the world where mothers believe it a duty to drown their children, and that eastern potentates openly deride the king of England for having only one wife instead of one hundred. There is no avoiding illiberality, under this belief,--as the philosopher understands illiberality. There is no avoiding the conclusion that the people who practice infanticide and polygamy are desperately wicked; and that minor differences of conduct are, abroad as at home, so many sins.

The observer who sets out with a more philosophical belief, not only escapes the affliction of seeing sin wherever he sees difference, and avoids the suffering of contempt and alienation from his species, but, by being prepared for what he witnesses, and aware of the causes, is free from the agitation of being shocked and alarmed, preserves his calmness, his hope, his sympathy; and is thus far better fitted to perceive, understand, and report upon the morals and manners of the people he visits. His more philosophical belief, derived from all fair evidence and just reflection, is, that every man's feelings of right and wrong, instead of being born with him, grow up in him from the influences to which he is subjected. We see that in other cases,--with regard to science, to art, and to the appearances of nature,--feelings grow out of knowledge and experience; and there is every evidence that it is so with regard to morals. The feelings begin very early; and this is the reason why they are supposed to be born with men; but they are few and imperfect in childhood, and, in the case of those who are strongly exercised in morals, they go on enlarging and strengthening and refining through life. See the effect upon the traveller's observations of his holding this belief about conscience! Knowing that some influences act upon the minds of all people in all countries, he looks everywhere for certain feelings of right and wrong which are as sure to be in all men's minds as if they were born with them. For instance, to torment another without any reason, real or imaginary, is considered wrong all over the world. In the same manner, to make others happy is universally considered right. At the same time, the traveller is prepared to find an infinite variety of differences in smaller matters, and is relieved from the necessity of pronouncing each to be a vice in one party or another. His own moral education having been a more elevated and advanced one than that of some of the people he contemplates, he cannot but feel sorrow and disgust at various things that he witnesses; but it is ignorance and barbarism that he mourns, and not vice. When he sees the Arab or American Indian offer daughter or wife to the stranger, as a part of the hospitality which is, in the host's mind, the first of duties, the observer regards the fact as he regards the mode of education in old Sparta, where physical hardihood and moral slavery constituted a man most honorable. If he sees an American student spend the whole of his small fortune, on leaving college, in travelling in Europe, he will not blame him as he would blame a young Englishman for doing the same thing. The Englishman would be a spendthrift; the American is wise: and the reason is, that their circumstances, prospects, and therefore their views of duty, are different. The American, being sure of obtaining an independent maintenance, may make the enlargement of his mind, and the cultivation of his tastes by travel, his first object; while the conscientious Englishman must fulfill the hard conditions of independence before he can travel. Capital is to him one of the chief requisites of honest independence; while to the American it is in the outset no requisite at all. To go without clothing was, till lately, perfectly innocent in the South Sea Islands; but now that civilization has been fairly established by the missionaries, it has become a sin. To let an enemy escape with his life is a disgrace in some countries of the world; while in others it is held more honorable to forgive than to punish him. Instances of such varieties and oppositions of conscience might be multiplied till they filled a volume, to the perplexity and grief of the unphilosophical, and the serene instruction of the philosophical observer.

The general influences under which universal ideas and feelings of right and wrong are formed, are dispensed by the Providence under which all are educated. That man should be happy is so evidently the intention of his Creator, the contrivances to that end are so multitudinous and so striking, that the perception of the aim may be called universal. Whatever tends to make men happy, becomes a fulfillment of the will of God. Whatever tends to make them miserable, becomes opposition to his will. There are, and must be, a host of obstacles to the express recognition of, and practical obedience to, these great principles; but they may be discovered as the root of religion and morals in all countries. There are impediments from ignorance, and consequent error, selfishness, and passion: the most infantile men mistake the means of human happiness, and the wisest have but a dim and fluctuating perception of them: but yet all men entertain one common conviction, that what makes people happy is good and right, and that what makes them miserable is evil and wrong. This conviction is at the bottom of practices which seem the most inconsistent with it. When the Ashantee offers a human sacrifice, it is in order to secure blessings from his gods. When the Hindoo exposes his sick parent in the Ganges, he thinks he is putting him out of pain by a charmed death. When Sand stabbed Kotzebue, he believed he was punishing and getting rid of an enemy and an obstacle to the welfare of his nation. When the Georgian planter buys and sells slaves, he goes on the supposition that he is preserving the order and due subordination of society. All these notions are shown by philosophy to be narrow, superficial, and mistaken. They have been outgrown by many, and are doubtless destined to be outgrown by all; but, acted upon by the ignorant and deluded, they are very different from the wickedness which is perpetrated against better knowledge. But these things would be wickedness, perpetrated against better knowledge, if the supposition of a universal, infallible Moral Sense were true. The traveller who should consistently adhere to the notion of a Moral Sense, must pronounce the

Ashantee worshipper as guilty as Greenacre: the Hindoo son a parricide, not only in fact, but in the most revolting sense of the term: Sand, a Thurtell: and the Georgian planter such a monster of tyranny as a Sussex farmer would be if he set up a whipping-post for his laborers, and sold their little ones to gypsies. Such judgments would be cruelly illiberal. The traveller who is furnished with the more accurate philosophy of Conscience would arrive at conclusions, not only more correct, but far less painful; and, without any laxity of principle, far more charitable.

So much for one instance of the advantage to the traveller of being provided with definite principles, to be used as a rallying point and test of his observations, instead of mere vague moral notions and general prepossessions, which can serve only as a false medium, by which much that he sees must necessarily be perverted or obscured.

Section 4

The traveller having satisfied himself that there are some universal feelings about right and wrong, and that in consequence some parts of human conduct are guided by general rules, must next give his attention to modes of conduct, which seem to him good or bad, prevalent in a nation, or district, or society of smaller limits. His first general principle is, that the law of nature is the only one by which mankind at large can be judged. His second must be, that every prevalent virtue or vice is the result of the particular circumstances amidst which the society exists.

The circumstances in which a prevalent virtue or vice originates, may or may not be traceable by a traveller. If traceable, he should spare no pains to make himself acquainted with the whole case. If obscure, he must beware of imputing disgraces to individuals, as if those individuals were living under the influences which have made himself what he is. He will not blame a deficiency of moral independence in a citizen of Philadelphia so severely as in a citizen of London; seeing, as he must do, that the want of moral independence is a prevalent fault in the United States, and that there must be some reason for it. Again, he will not look to the Polish peasant for the political intelligence, activity, and principle which delight him in the log-house of the American farmer. He sees that Polish peasants are generally supine, and American farmers usually interested about politics; and that there must be reasons for the difference.

In a majority of cases such reasons are, to a great extent, ascertainable. In Spain, for instance, there is a large class of wretched and irretrievable beggars; and their idleness, dirt, and lying trouble the very soul of the traveller. What is the reason of the prevalence of this degraded class and of its vices? A Court Lady[C] wrote, in ancient days, piteous complaints of the poverty of the sovereign, the nobility, the army, and the destitute ladies who waited upon the queen. The sovereign could not give his attendants their dinners; the nobility melted down their plate and sold their jewels; the soldiers were famishing in garrison, so that the young deserted, and the aged and invalids wasted away, actually starved to death. The lady mentions with surprise, that a particularly large amount of gold and silver had arrived from the foreign possessions of Spain that year, and tries to account for the universal misery by saying that a great proportion of these riches was appropriated by merchants who supplied the Spaniards with the necessaries of life from abroad; and she speaks of this as an evil. She is an example of an unphilosophical observer,--one who could not be trusted to report--much less to account for--the morals and manners of the people before her eyes. What says a philosophical observer?[D] "Spain and Portugal, the countries which possess the mines, are, after Poland, perhaps the two most beggarly countries in Europe."--"Their trade to their colonies is carried on in their own ships, and is much greater" (than their foreign commerce,) "on account of the great riches and extent of those colonies. But it has never introduced any considerable manufactures for distant sale into either of those countries, and the greater part of both remains uncultivated."--"The proportion of gold and silver to the annual produce of the land and labor of Spain is said to be very considerable, and that you frequently find there a profusion of plate in houses where there is nothing else which would in other countries be thought suitable or correspondent to this sort of magnificence. The cheapness of gold and silver, or, what is the same thing, the dearness of all commodities, which is the necessary effect of this redundance of the precious metals, discourages both the agriculture and manufactures of Spain and Portugal, and enables foreign nations to supply them with many sorts of rude, and with almost all sorts of manufactured produce, for a smaller quantity of gold and silver than what they themselves can either raise or make them for at home."--When it is considered that in Spain gold and silver are called wealth, and that there is little other; that manufactures and commerce scarcely exist; that agriculture is discouraged, and that therefore there is a lack of occupation for the lower classes, it may be fairly concluded that the idle upper orders will be found lazy, proud, and poor; the idle lower classes in a state of beggary; and that the most virtuous and happy part of the population will be those who are engaged in tilling the soil, and in the occupations which are absolutely necessary in towns. One may see with the mind's eye the groups of intriguing grandees, who have no business on their estates to occupy their time and thoughts; or the crowd of hungry beggars, thronging round the door of a convent, to

23

receive the daily alms; or the hospitable and courteous peasants, of whom a traveller[E] says, "There is a civility to strangers, and an easy style of behavior familiar to this class of Spanish society, which is very remote from the churlish and awkward manners of the English and German peasantry. Their sobriety and endurance of fatigue are very remarkable; and there is a constant cheerfulness in their demeanor which strongly prepossesses a stranger in their favor."--"I should be glad if I could, with justice, give as favorable a picture of the higher orders of society in this country; but, perhaps, when we consider their wretched education, and their early habits of indolence and dissipation, we ought not to wonder at the state of contempt and degradation to which they are reduced. I am not speaking the language of prejudice, but the result of the observations I have made, in which every accurate observer among our countrymen has concurred with me, in saying that the figures and countenances of the higher orders are as much inferior to those of the peasants, as their moral qualities are in the view I have given of them."--All this might be foreseen to be unavoidable in a country where the means of living are passively derived from abroad, and where the honor and rewards of successful industry are confined to a class of the community. The mines should bear the blame of the prevalent faults of the saucy beggars and beggarly grandees of Spain.

To anyone who has at all considered at home the bearings of a social system which is grounded upon physical force, or those of the opposite arrangements which rely upon moral power, it can be no mystery abroad that there should be prevalent moral characteristics among the subjects of such systems; and the vices which exist under them will be, however mourned, leniently judged. Take the Feudal System as an instance, first, and then its opposite. A little thought makes it clear what virtues and vices will be almost certain to subsist under the influences of each.

The baron lives in his castle, on a rock or some other eminence, whence he can overlook his domains, or where his ancestor reared his abode for purposes of safety. During this stage of society there is little domestic refinement and comfort. The furniture is coarse; the library is not tempting; and the luxurious ease of cities is out of the question. The pleasures of the owner lie abroad. There he devotes himself to rough sports, and enjoys his darling luxury,--the exercise of power. Within the dwelling the wife and her attendants spend their lives in handiworks, in playing with the children and keeping them in order, in endless conversation on the few events which come under their notice, and in obedience to and companionship with the priest. While the master is hunting, or gathering together his retainers for the feast, the women are spinning or sewing, gossiping, confessing, or doing penance; while the priest studies in his apartment, shares in the mirth, or soothes the troubles of the household, and rules the mind of the noble by securing the confidence of his wife. Out of doors, there are the retainers, by whatever name they may be called. Their poor dwellings are crowded round the castle of the lord; their patches of arable land lie nearest, and the pastures beyond; that, at least, the supply of human food may be secured from any enemy. These portions of land are held on a tenure of service; and, as the retainers have no property in them, and no interest in their improvement, and are, moreover, liable to be called away from their tillage at any moment, to perform military or other service, the soil yields sorry harvests, and the lean cattle are not very ornamental to the pastures. The wives of the peasantry are often left, at an hour's warning, in the unprotected charge of their half-clothed and untaught children, as well as of the cattle and the field.--The festivals of the people are on holy days, and on the return of the chief from war, or from a pre-eminent chase.

Now, what must be the morals of such a district as this? and, it may be added, of the whole country of which it forms a part? for, if there be one feudal settlement of the kind, there must be more; and the society is in fact made up of a certain number of complete sets of persons,--of establishments like this.--There is no need to go back some centuries for an original to the picture: it exists in more than one country in Europe now.

This kind of society is composed of two classes only; those who have something, and those who have nothing. The chief has property, some knowledge, and great power. With individual differences, the chiefs may be expected to be imperious, from their liberty and indulgence of will; brave, from their exposure to toil and danger; contemptuous of men, from their own supremacy; superstitious, from the influence of the priest in the household; lavish, from the permanency of their property; vain of rank and personal distinction, from the absence of pursuits unconnected with self; and hospitable, partly from the same cause, and partly from their own hospitality being the only means of gratifying their social dispositions.

The clergy will be politic, subservient, studious, or indolent, kind-hearted, effeminate, with a strong tendency to spiritual pride, and love of spiritual dominion. It will be surprising, too, if they are not driven into infidelity by the credulity of their pupils.

The women will be ignorant and superstitious, for want of varied instruction; brave, from the frequent presence or promise of danger; efficient, from the small division of labor which is practicable in the superintendence of such a family; given to gossip and uncertainty of temper, from the sameness of their lives; devoted to their husbands and children, from the absence of all other important objects; and vain of such accomplishments as they have, from an ignorance of what remains to be achieved.

The retainers must be ignorant, --physically strong and imposing, perhaps, but infants in mind, and slaves in morals. Their worship is idolatry--of their chief. The virtues permitted to them are fidelity, industry, domestic attachment, and sobriety. It is difficult to see what others are possible. Their faults are all comprehended in the word barbarism.

These characteristics may be extended to the divisions of the nation corresponding to those of the household: for the sovereign is only a higher feudal chief: his nobles are a more exalted sort of serfs; and those who are masters at home become slaves at court. Under this system, who would be so hardy as to treat brutality in a serf, cunning in a priest, prejudice in a lady, and imperiousness in a lord, as anything but the results--inevitable as mournful--of the state of society?

Feudalism is founded upon physical force, and therefore bears a relation to the past alone. Right begins in might, and all the social relations of men have originated in physical superiority. The most prevalent ideas of the feudal period arise out of the past; what has been longest honored is held most honorable; and the understanding of men, unexercised by learning, and undisciplined by society and political action, falls back upon precedent, and reposes there. The tastes, and even the passions, of the feudal period bear a relation to antiquity. Ambition, prospective as it is in its very nature, has, in this case, a strong retrospective character. The glory that the descendant derives from his fathers, he burns to transmit. The past is everything: the future, except in as far as it may resemble the past, is nothing.

Such, with modifications, have been the prevalent ideas, tastes, and passions of the civilized world, till lately. The opposite state of society, which has begun to be realized, occasions prevalent ideas, and therefore prevalent virtues and vices, of an opposite character.

As commerce enlarges, as other professions besides the clerical arise, as trades become profitable, as cities swell in importance, as communication improves, raising villages into towns, and hamlets into villages, and the affairs of central communities become spread through the circumference, the lower classes rise, the chiefs lose much of their importance, the value of men for their intrinsic qualifications is discovered, and such men take the lead in managing the affairs of associated citizens. Instead of all being done by orders issued from a central power,--commands carrying forth an imperious will, and bringing back undoubting obedience,--social affairs begin to be managed by the heads and hands of the parties immediately interested. Self-government in municipal affairs takes place; and, having taken place in any one set of circumstances, it appears likely to be employed within a wider and a wider range, till all the government of the community is of that character. The United States are the most remarkable examples now before the world of the reverse of the feudal system,--its principles, its methods, its virtues and vices.

In as far as the Americans revert, in ideas and tastes, to the past, this may be attributed to the transition being not yet perfected,--to the generation which organized the republic having been educated amidst the remains of feudalism. There are still Americans who boast of ancestors high in the order of birth rather than of merit; who in talking of rank have ideas of birth in their minds, and whose tastes lie in the past. But such will be the case while the literature of the world breathes the spirit of former ages, and softens the transition to an opposite social state. A new literature, new modes of thought, are daily arising, which point more and more towards the future. We have already records of the immediate state of the minds and fortunes of men and of communities, and not a few speculations which stretch far forward into the future. Every year is the admission more extensively entered into that moral power is nobler than physical force; there is more earnestness in the conferences of nations, and less proneness to war. The highest creations of literature itself, however long ago produced, are now discovered to bear as close a relation to the future as the past. They are for all time, through all its changes. While pillars of light in the dim regions of antiquity, they pass over in the dawn, and are still before us, casting their shadows to our feet as guides into the dazzling future. Pre-eminent among them is the Book which never had any retrospective character in it. It never sanctioned physical force, pride of ancestry, of valor, of influence, or any other pride. It never sanctioned arbitrary division of ranks. It never lauded the virtues of feudalism in their disconnection with other virtues; it never spared the faults of feudalism, on the ground of their being the necessary product of feudal circumstances; neither does it now laud and tolerate the virtues and vices developed by democracy. This guide has never yet taken up its rest. It is in advance of all existing democracies, as it ever was of all despotisms. The fact is, that, while all manifestations of eminent intellectual and moral force have an imperishable quality, this supreme book has not only an immortal freshness, but bears no relation to time:--to it "one day is as a thousand years, and a thousand years as one day."

What are the prevalent virtues and faults which are to be looked for in the future,--or in those countries which represent somewhat of the future, as others afford a weakened image of the past? What allowance is the traveller in America to make? Almost precisely the reverse of what he would make in Russia.

In-door luxury has succeeded to out-door sports: the mechanical arts flourish from the elevation of the lower classes, and prowess is gone out of fashion. The consequence of this is that the traveller sees ostentation of personal luxury instead of retinue. In the course of transition to the time when merit will constitute the highest claim to rank, wealth succeeds to birth: but even already, the claims of wealth give way before those of intellect. The popular author has more observance than the millionaire in the United States. This is honorable, and yields promise of a still better graduation of ranks. Where moral force is recognized as the moving power of society, it seems to follow that the condition of Woman must be elevated; that new pursuits will be opened to her, and a wider and stronger discipline be afforded to her powers. It is not so in America; but this is owing to the interference of other circumstances with the full operation of democratic principles. The absence of an aristocratic or a sovereign will impels men to find some other will on which to repose their individual weakness, and with which to employ their human veneration. The will of the majority becomes their refuge and unwritten law. The few free-minded resist this will, when it is in opposition to their own, and the slavish many submit. This is accordingly found to be the most conspicuous fault of the Americans. Their cautious subservience to public opinion,--their deficiency of moral independence,--is the crying sin of their society. Again, the social equality by which the whole of life is laid open to all in a democratic republic, in which every man who has power in him may attain all to which that power is a requisite, cannot but enhance the importance of each in the eyes of all; and the consequence is a mutual respect and deference, and also a mutual helpfulness, which are in themselves virtues of a high order, and preparatives for others. In these the Americans are exercised and accomplished to a degree never generally attained in any other country. This class of virtues constitutes their distinguishing honor, their crowning grace in the company of nations.--Activity and ingenuity are a matter of course where every man's lot is in his own hands. Unostentatious hospitality and charity might, in some democracies, be likely to languish; but the Americans have the wealth of a young country, and the warmth of a young national existence, as stimulus and warrant for pecuniary liberality of every kind.--Popular vanity, and the subservience of political representatives, are the chief dangers which remain to be alluded to; and there will probably be no republic for ages where these will not be found in the form of prevalent vices.--If, under a feudal system, there is a wholesome exercise of reverence in the worship of ancestry, there is, under the opposite system, a no less salutary and perpetual impulse to generosity in the care for posterity. The one has been, doubtless, a benignant influence, tempering the ruggedness and violence of despotism; the other will prove an elevating force, lifting men above the personal selfishness and mutual subservience which are the besetting perils of equals who unite to govern by their common will.

Whatever may be his philosophy of individual character, the reflective observer cannot travel, with his mind awake, without admitting that there can be no question but that national character is formed, or largely influenced, by the gigantic circumstances which, being the product of no individual mind, are directly attributable to the great Moral Governor of the human race. Every successive act of research or travel will impress him more and more deeply with this truth, which, for the sake of his own peace and liberality, it would be well that he should carry about with him from the outset. He will not visit individuals with any bitterness of censure for participating in prevalent faults. He will regard social virtues and graces as shedding honor on all whom they overshadow, from the loftiest to the lowliest; while he is not disposed to indulge contempt, or anything but a mild compassion, for any social depravity or deformity which, being the clear result of circumstances, and itself a circumstance, may be considered as surely destined to be remedied, as the wisdom of associated, like that of individual man, grows with his growth, and strengthens with his strength.

Chapter 2: Moral Requisites

I respect knowledge; but I do not despise ignorance.
They think only as their fathers thought, worship as
they worshipped. They do no more.

--Rogers

He was alive To all that was enjoyed
where'er he went, And all that was endured.

--Wordsworth

The traveller, being furnished with the philosophical requisites for the observation of morals and manners,

1stly. With a certainty of what it is that he wants to know,--

2ndly. With principles which may serve as a rallying point and test of his observations,--

3rdly. With, for instance, a philosophical and definite, instead of a popular and vague, notion about the origin of human feelings of right and wrong,--

4thly. And with a settled conviction that prevalent virtues and vices are the result of gigantic general influences,--is yet not fitted for his object if certain moral requisites be wanting in him.

An observer, to be perfectly accurate, should be himself perfect. Every prejudice, every moral perversion, dims or distorts whatever the eye looks upon. But as we do not wait to be perfect before we travel, we must content ourselves with discovering, in order to avoidance, what would make our task hopeless, and how we may put ourselves in a state to learn at least something truly. We cannot suddenly make ourselves a great deal better than we have been, for such an object as observing Morals and Manners; but, by clearly ascertaining what it is that the most commonly, or the most grossly, vitiates foreign observation, we may put a check upon our spirit of prejudice, and carry with us restoratives of temper and spirits which may be of essential service to us in our task.

The observer must have sympathy; and his sympathy must be untrammelled and unreserved. If a traveller be a geological inquirer, he may have a heart as hard as the rocks he shivers, and yet succeed in his immediate objects: if he be a student of the fine arts, he may be as silent as a picture, and yet gain his ends: if he be a statistical investigator, he may be as abstract as a column of figures, and yet learn what he wants to know: but an observer of morals and manners will be liable to deception at every turn, if he does not find his way to hearts and minds. Nothing was ever more true than that "as face answers to face in water, so is the heart of man." To the traveller there are two meanings in this wise saying, both worthy of his best attention. It means that the action of the heart will meet a corresponding action, and that the nature of the heart will meet a corresponding nature. Openness and warmth of heart will be greeted with openness and warmth:--this is one truth. Hearts, generous or selfish, pure or gross, gay or sad, will understand, and therefore be likely to report of, only their like:--this is another truth.

There is the same human heart everywhere,--the universal growth of mind and life,--ready to open to the sunshine of sympathy, flourishing in the enclosures of cities, and blossoming wherever dropped in the wilderness; but folding up when touched by chill, and drooping in gloom. As well might the Erl-king go and play the florist in the groves and plains of the tropics, as an unsympathizing man render an account of society. It will all turn to stubble and sapless rigidity before his eyes.

There is the same human heart everywhere; and, if the traveller has a good one himself, he will presently find this out, whatever may have been his fears at home of checks to his sympathy from difference of education, objects in life, &c. There is no place where people do not suffer and enjoy; where love is not the high festival of life; where birth and death are not occasions of emotion; where parents are not proud of their boy-children; where thoughtful minds do not speculate upon the two eternities; where, in short, there is not broad ground on which any two human beings may meet and clasp hands, if they have but unsophisticated hearts. If a man have not sympathy, there is no point of the universe--none so wide even as the Mahomedan bridge over the bottomless pit--where he can meet with his fellow. Such an one is indeed floundering in the bottomless pit, with only the shadows of men ever flitting about him.

I have mentioned elsewhere, what will well bear repetition,--that an American merchant, who had made several voyages to China, dropped a remark by his own fire-side on the narrowness which causes us to conclude, avowedly or silently, that, however well men may use the light they have, they cannot be more than nominally our brethren, unless they have our religion, our philosophy, and our methods of attaining both. He said he often recurred, with delight, to the conversations he had enjoyed with his Chinese friends on some of the highest speculative, and some of the deepest and widest practical subjects, which his fellow-citizens of New England were apt to think could be the business only of Protestant Christians. This American merchant's observations on oriental morals and manners had an incalculable weight after he had said this; for it was known that he had seen into hearts, as well as met faces, and discovered what people's minds were busy about, as their hands were pursuing the universal employment of earning their subsistence.

Unless a traveller interprets by his sympathies what he sees, he cannot but misunderstand the greater part of that which comes under his observation. He will not be admitted with freedom into the retirements of domestic life; the instructive commentary on all the facts of life,--discourse,--will be of a slight and superficial character. People will talk to him of the things they care least about, instead of seeking his sympathy about the affairs which are deepest in their hearts. He will be amused with public spectacles, and informed of historical and chronological facts; but he will not be invited to weddings and christenings; he will hear no love-tales; domestic sorrows will be kept as secrets from him; the old folks will not pour out their stories to him, nor the children bring him their prattle. Such a traveller will be no more fitted to report on morals and manners than he would be to give an account of the silver mines of Siberia by walking over the surface, and seeing the entrance and the product.

"Human conduct," says a philosopher, "is guided by rules." Without these rules, men could not live together, and they are also necessary to the repose of individual minds. Robinson Crusoe could not have endured his life for a month without rules to live by. A life without purpose is uncomfortable enough; but a life without rules would be a wretchedness which, happily, man is not constituted to bear. The rules by which men live are chiefly drawn from the universal convictions about right and wrong which I have mentioned as being formed everywhere, under strong general influences. When sentiment is connected with these rules, they become religion; and this religion is the animating spirit of all that is said and done. If the stranger cannot sympathize in the sentiment, he cannot understand the religion; and without understanding the religion, he cannot appreciate the spirit of words and acts. A stranger who has never felt any strong political interest, and cannot sympathize with American sentiment about the majesty of social equality, and the beauty of mutual government, can never understand the political religion of the United States; and the sayings of the citizens by their own fire-sides, the perorations of orators in town-halls, the installations of public servants, and the process of election, will all be empty sound and grimace to him. He will be tempted to laugh,--to call the world about him mad,--like one who, without hearing the music, sees a room-full of people begin to dance. The case is the same with certain Americans who have no antiquarian sympathies, and who think our sovereigns mad for riding to St. Stephen's in the royal state-coach, with eight horses covered with trappings, and a tribe of grotesque footmen. I have found it an effort of condescension to inform such observers that we should not think of inventing such a coach and appurtenances at the present day, any more than we should the dress of the Christ-Hospital boys. If an unsympathizing stranger is so perplexed by a mere matter of external arrangement,--a royal procession, or a popular election,--what can he be expected to make of that which is far more important, more intricate, more mysterious,--neighborly and domestic life? If he knows and feels nothing of the religion of these, he could learn but little about them, even if the roofs of all the houses of a city were made transparent to him, and he could watch all that is done in every parlor, kitchen, and nursery in a circuit of five miles.

What strange scenes and transactions must such an one think that there are in the world! What would he have thought of the spectacle one day seen in Hayti, when Toussaint L'Ouverture ranged his negro forces before him, called out thirteen men from the ranks by name, and ordered them to repair to a certain spot to be immediately shot? What would he have thought of these thirteen men for crossing their arms upon their breasts, bowing their heads submissively, and yielding instant obedience? He might have pronounced Toussaint a ferocious despot, and the thirteen so many craven fools: while the facts wear a very different aspect to one who knows the minds of the men. It was necessary to the good-will of a society but lately organized out of chaos, to make no distinction between negro and other insurgents; and these thirteen men were ringleaders in a revolt, Toussaint's nephew being one of them. This accounts for the general's share in the transaction. As for the negroes, the General was also the Deliverer,--an object of worship to people of his color. Obedience to him was a rule, exalted by every sentiment of gratitude, awe, admiration, pride, and love, into a religion; and a Haytian of that day would no more have thought of resisting a command of Toussaint, than of disputing a thunder-stroke or an earthquake.--What would an unsympathizing observer make of the Paschal supper, as celebrated in the houses of Hebrews throughout the world,--of the care not to break a bone of the lamb,--of the company all standing, the men girded and shod as for a journey, and the youngest child of the household invariably asking what this is all for? What would the observer call it but mummery, if he had no feeling for the awful traditional and religious emotion involved in the symbol?--What would such an one think of the terrified flight of two Spanish nobles from the wrath of

33

their sovereign, incurred by their having saved his beloved queen from being killed by a fall from her horse? What a puzzle is here,--even when all the facts of the case are known;--that the king was looking from a balcony to see his queen mount her Andalusian horse: that the horse reared, plunged, and bolted, throwing the queen, whose foot was entangled in the stirrup: that she was surrounded with gentlemen who stood aloof, because by the law of Spain it was death to any but her little pages to touch the person, and especially the foot of the queen, and her pages were too young to rescue her; that these two gentlemen devoted themselves to save her; and having caught the horse, and extricated the royal foot, fled for their lives from the legal wrath of the king! Whence such a law? From the rule that the queen of Spain has no legs. Whence such a rule? From the meaning that the queen of Spain is a being too lofty to touch the earth. Here we come at last to the sentiment of loyal admiration and veneration which sanctifies the law and the rule, and interprets the incident. To a heartless stranger the whole appears a mere solemn absurdity, fit only to be set aside, as it was apparently by pardon from the king being obtained by the instant intercession of the queen. But in the eyes of every Spaniard the transaction was, in all its parts, as far from absurdity as the danger of the two nobles was real and pressing.--Again, what can a heartless observer understand by the practice, almost universal in the world, of celebrating the naming of children? The Christian parent employs a form by which the infant is admitted as a lamb of Christ's flock: the Chinese father calls his kindred together to witness the conferring first of the surname, and then of "the milk-name,"--some endearing diminutive, to cease with infancy: the Moslem consults an astrologer before giving a name to his child: and the savage selects a name-sake for his infant from among the beasts or birds, with whose characteristic quality he would fain endow his offspring. What a general rule is here, exalted by a universal sentiment into an act of religion! The ceremonial observed in each case is widely different in its aspect to one who sees in it merely a cumbrous way of transacting a matter of convenience, and to another who perceives in it the initiation of a new member into the family of mankind, and a looking forward to,--an attempt to make provision for, the future destiny of an unconscious and helpless being.

Thus it will be through the whole range of the traveller's observation. If he be full of sympathy, everything he sees will be instructive, and the most important matters will be the most clearly revealed. If he be unsympathizing, the most important things will be hidden from him, and symbols (in which every society abounds) will be only absurd or trivial forms. The stranger will be wise to conclude, when he sees anything seriously done which appears to him insignificant or ludicrous, that there is more in it than he perceives, from some deficiency of knowledge or feeling of his own.

The other way in which heart is found to answer to heart is too obvious to require to be long dwelt upon. Men not only see according to the light they shed from their own breasts,--whether it be the sunshine of generosity or the hell-flames of bad passions,--but they attract to themselves spirits like their own. The very same persons appear very differently to a traveller who calls into exercise all their best qualities, and to one who has an affinity with their worst: but it is a yet more important consideration that actually different elements of society will range themselves round the observer according to the skepticism or faith of his temper, the purity or depravity of his tastes, and the elevation or insignificance of his objects. The Americans, somewhat nettled with the injustice of English travellers' reports of their country, have jokingly proposed to take lodgings in Wapping for some thorough-bred American vixen, of low tastes and coarse manners, and employ her to write an account of English morals and manners from what she might see in a year's abode in the choice locality selected for her. This would be no great exaggeration of the process of observation of foreigners which is perpetually going on.

What should gamesters know of the philanthropists of the society they pass through? or the profligate, of the real state of domestic life? What can the moral skeptic report of religious or philosophical confessorship in any nation? or the sordid trader, of the higher kinds of intellectual cultivation? or the dandy, of the extent and administration of charity? It may be said that neither can the philanthropic traveller--the missionary--see otherwise than partially for want of "knowledge of the world;" that persons of sober habits can learn nothing that is going on in the moral depths of society; and the good are actually scoffed at for their absence from many scenes of human life, and their supposed ignorance of many things in human nature. But it is certain that the best part of every man's mind is far more a specimen of himself than the worst; and that the characteristics of a society, in like manner, are to be traced in the wisest and most genial of its pervading ideas and common transactions, instead of those disgraceful ones which are common to all. Swindlers, drunkards, people of low tastes and bad passions, are found in every country, and nowhere characterize a nation; while the reverence of man in America, the pursuit of speculative truth in Germany, philanthropic enterprise in France, love of freedom in Switzerland, popular education in China, domestic purity in Norway,--each of these great moral beauties is a star on the forehead of a nation. Goodness and simplicity are indissolubly united. The bad are the most sophisticated, all the world over; and the good the least. It may be taken as a rule that the best qualities of a people, as of an individual, are the most characteristic--(what is really best being tested, not by prejudice, but principle). He has the best chance of ascertaining these best qualities who has them in himself; and he who has them not may as well pretend to give a picture of a metropolitan city by showing a map of its drainage, as report of a nation after an intercourse with its knaves and its profligates. To stand on the highest pinnacle is the best way of obtaining an accurate general view, in contemplating a society as well as a city.

Chapter 3: Mechanical Requisites

He travels and expatiates, as the bee
From flower to flower, so he from land to land:
The manners, customs, policy, of all
Pay contribution to the stores he gleans.

--The Task

Thy speaking of my tongue, and I thine, most truly falsely,
must needs be granted to be much at one.

--King Henry V

No philosophical or moral fitness will qualify a traveller to observe a people if he does not select a mode of travelling which will enable him to see and converse with a great number and variety of persons. An ambassador has no chance of learning much of the people he visits anywhere but in a new country like America. While he is en route, he is too stately in appearance to allow of any familiarity on the part of the people by the road-side. His carriages might almost as well roll through a city of the dead, for anything he will learn from intercourse with the living. The case is not much better when a family or a party of friends travel together on the Continent, committing the business of the expedition to servants, and shrinking from intercourse, on all social occasions, with English shyness or pride.

The behavior of the English on the Continent has become a matter of very serious consequence to the best informed and best mannered of their countrymen, as it has long been to the natives into whose society they may happen to fall. I have heard gentlemen say that they lose half their pleasure in going abroad, from the coldness and shyness with which the English are treated; a coldness and shyness which they think fully warranted by the conduct of their predecessors in travel. I have heard ladies say that they find great difficulty in becoming acquainted with their neighbors at the tables-d'hôte; and that, when they have succeeded, an apology for the reluctance to converse has been offered, in the form of explanation that English travellers generally "appear to dislike being spoken to" so much as to render it a matter of civility to leave them alone. The travelling arrangements of the English seem designed to cut them off from companionship with the people they go to see; and they preclude the possibility of studying morals and manners in a way which is perfectly ludicrous to persons of a more social temperament and habits.

A good deal may be learned on board steam-boats, and in such vehicles as the American stages; and when accommodations of the kind become common, it will be difficult for the sulkiest Englishman to avoid admitting some ideas into his mind from the conversation and actions of the groups around him. When steam-boats ply familiarly on the Indus, and we have the rail-road to Calcutta which people are joking about, and another across the Pampas,--when we make trips to New Zealand, and think little of a run down the west coast of Africa,--places where we shall go for fashion's sake, and cannot go boxed up in a carriage of Long Acre origin,--our countrymen will, perforce, exchange conversation with the persons they meet, and may chance to get rid of the unsociability for which they are notorious, and by which they cast a veil over hearts and faces, and a shadow over their own path, wherever they go.

Meantime, the wisest and happiest traveller is the pedestrian. If gentlemen and ladies want to see pictures, let them post to Florence, and be satisfied with learning what they can from the windows by the way. But if they want to see either scenery or people, let all who have strength and courage go on foot. I prefer this even to horseback. A horse is an anxiety and a trouble. Something is sure to ail it; and one is more anxious about its accommodation than about one's own. The pedestrian traveller is wholly free from care. There is no such freeman on earth as he is for the time. His amount of toil is usually within his own choice,--in any civilized region. He can go on and stop when he likes: if a fit of indolence overtakes him, he can linger for a day or a week in any spot that pleases him. He is not whirled past a beautiful view almost before he has seen it. He is not tantalized by the idea that from this or that point he could see something still finer, if he could but reach it. He can reach almost every point his wishes wander to. The pleasure is indescribable of saying to one's self, "I will go there,"--"I will rest yonder,"--and forthwith accomplishing it. He can sit on a rock in the midst of a rushing stream as often in a day as he likes. He can hunt a waterfall by its sound; a sound which the carriage-wheels prevent other travellers from hearing. He can follow out any tempting glade in any wood. There is no cushion of moss at the foot of an old tree that he may not sit down on if he pleases. He can read for an hour without fear of passing by something unnoticed while his eyes are fixed upon his book. His food is welcome, be its quality what it may, while he eats it under the alders in some recess of a brook. He is secure of his sleep, be his chamber ever so sordid; and when his waking eyes rest upon his knapsack, his heart leaps with pleasure as he remembers where he is, and what a day is before him. Even the weather seems to be of less consequence to the pedestrian than to other travellers. A pedestrian journey presupposes abundance of time, so that the traveller can rest in villages on rainy days, and in the shade of a wood during the hours when the sun is too powerful. And if he prefers not waiting for the rain, it is not the evil to him that it would be in cities and in the pursuit of business. The only evil of rain that I know of, to healthy persons in exercise, is that it spoils the clothes; and the clothes of a pedestrian traveller are not usually of a spoilable quality. Rain does not deform the face of things everywhere as it does in a city. It adds a new aspect of beauty occasionally to a wood, to mountains, to lake and ocean scenery. I remember a hale, cheerful pedestrian tourist whom we met frequently among the White Mountains of New Hampshire, and whom we remarked as being always the briskest of the company at the hotel table in the evening, and the merriest at breakfast. He had the best of it one day, when we passed him in Franconia Defile, after a heavy rain had set in. We were packed in a wagon which seemed likely to fill with water before we got to our destination; and miserable enough we looked, drenched and cold. The traveller was marching on over the rocky road, his book safe in its oil-skin cover, and his clothes-bag similarly protected; his face bright and glowing with exercise, and his summer jacket of linen feeling, as he told us, all the pleasanter for being wet through. As he passed each recess of the defile, he looked up perpetually to see the rain come smoking out of the fissures of the rocks; and when he reached the opening by which he was to descend to the plain, he stood still, to watch the bar of dewy yellow light which lay along the western sky where the sun had just set. He looked just as happy on other days. Sometimes we passed him lying along on a hill side; sometimes talking with a family at the door of a log-house; sometimes reading as he walked under the shade of the forest. I, for one, often longed to dismiss our wagon or barouche, and to follow his example.

One peculiar advantage of pedestrian travelling is the pleasure of a gradual approach to celebrated or beautiful places. Every turn of the road gains in interest; every object that meets the eye seems to have some initiative meaning; and when the object itself at last appears, nothing can surpass the delight of flinging one's self on the ground to rest upon the first impression, and to interpose a delicious pause before the final attainment. It is not the same thing to desire your driver to stop when you come to the point of view. The first time that I felt this was on a pedestrian tour in Scotland, when I was at length to see mountains. The imagination of myself and my companion had fixed strongly on Dunkeld, as being a scene of great beauty, and our first resting-place among the mountains. The sensation had been growing all the morning. Men, houses, and trees had seemed to be growing diminutive,--an irresistible impression to the novice in mountain scenery: the road began to follow the windings of the Tay, a sign that the plain was contracting into a pass. Beside a cistern, on a green bank of this pass, we had dined; a tract of heath next lay before us, and we traversed it so freshly and merrily as to be quite unaware that we were getting towards the end of our seventeen miles, though still conscious that the spirit of the mountains was upon us. We were deeply engaged in talk, when a winding of the road brought us in full view of the lovely scene which is known to all who have approached Dunkeld by the Perth road. We could scarcely believe that this was it, so soon. We turned to our map and guide-book, and found that we were standing on the site of Birnam wood; that Dunsinane hill was in sight, and that it was indeed the old cathedral tower of Dunkeld that rose so grandly among the beeches behind the bridge. We took such a long and fond gaze as I never enjoyed from a carriage window. If it was thus with an object of no more importance or difficulty of attainment than Dunkeld, what must it be to catch the first view of the mysterious temples that

> "Stand between the mountains and the sea;
> Awful memorials, but of whom we know not!"

or to survey from a height, at sunrise, the brook Kedron and the valley of Jehoshaphat!

What is most to our present purpose, however, is the consideration of the facilities afforded by pedestrian travelling for obtaining a knowledge of the people. We all remember Goldsmith's travels with his flute, his sympathies, his cordiality of heart and manner, and his reliance on the hospitality of the country people. Such an one as he is not bound to take up with such specimens as he may meet with by the side of the high road; he can penetrate into the recesses of the country, and drop into the hamlet among the hills, and the homesteads down the lanes, and now and then spend a day with the shepherd in his fold on the downs; he can stop where there is a festival, and solve many a perplexity by carrying over the conversation of one day into the intercourse of the next, with a fresh set of people; he can obtain access to almost every class of persons, and learn their own views of their own affairs. His opportunities are inestimable.

If it were a question which could learn most of Morals and Manners by travel,--the gentleman accomplished in philosophy and learning, proceeding in his carriage, with a courier,--or a simple pedestrian tourist, furnished only with the language, and with an open heart and frank manners,--I should have no doubt that the pedestrian would return more familiar with his subject than the other. If the wealthy scholar and philosopher could make himself a citizen of the world for the time, and go forth on foot, careless of luxury, patient of fatigue, and fearless of solitude, he would be not only of the highest order of tourists, but a benefactor to the highest kind of science; and he would become familiarized with what few are acquainted with,--the best pleasures, transient and permanent, of travel. Those who cannot pursue this method will achieve most by laying aside state, conversing with the people they fall in with, and diverging from the high road as much as possible.

Nothing need be said on a matter so obvious as the necessity of understanding the language of the people visited. Some familiarity with it must be attained before anything else can be done. It seems to be unquestioned, however, that a good deal of the unsociability of the English abroad is owing not so much to contempt of their neighbors, as to the natural pride which makes them shrink from attempting what they cannot do well. I am confident that we say much less than we feel about the awkwardness and constraint of our first self-committals to a foreign language. It is impossible but that everyone must feel the weight of the penalty of making himself ridiculous at every step, and of presenting a kind of false appearance of himself to everyone with whom he converses. A German gentleman in America, who has exactly that right degree of self-respect which enabled him to set strenuously about learning English, of which he did not understand a word, and who mastered it so completely as to lecture in faultless English at the end of two years, astonished a party of friends one day, persuaded as they were that they perfectly knew him, and that the smooth and deliberate flow of his beautiful language was a consequence of the calmness of his temper, and the philosophical character of his mind. A German woman with children came begging to the house while the party were at their dessert. The professor caught her tones when the door of the dining-room was open; he rushed into the hall, presently returned for a dish or two, and emptied the gingerbread, and other material of the dessert, into her lap. The company went out to see, and found the professor transformed; he was talking with a rapidity and vehemence which they had never supposed him capable of; and one of the party told me how sorry she felt, and has felt ever since, to think of the state of involuntary disguise in which he is living among those who would know him best. Difference of language is undeniably a cause of great suffering and difficulty, magnificent and incalculable as are its uses. It is no exception to the general rule that every great good involves some evil.

Happily, however, the difficulty may be presently so far surmounted as not to interfere with the object of observing Morals and Manners. Impossible as it may be to attain to an adequate expression of one's self in a foreign tongue, it is easy to most persons to learn to understand it perfectly when spoken by others. During this process, a common and almost unavoidable mistake is to suppose a too solemn and weighty meaning in what is expressed in an unfamiliar language. This arises partly from our having become first acquainted with the language in books; and partly from the meaning having been attained with effort, and seeming, by natural association, worth the pains. The first French dialogues which a child learns, seem more emphatic in their meanings than the same material would in English; and the student of German finds a grandeur in lines of Schiller, and in clauses of Herder's and Krummacher's Parables, which he looks for in vain when he is practiced in the language. It is well to bear this in mind on a first entrance into a foreign society, or the traveller may chance to detect himself treasuring up nonsense, and making much of mere trivialities, because they reached him clothed in the mystery of a strange language. He will be like lame Jervas, when he first came up from the mine in which he was born, caressing the weeds he had gathered by the road side, and refusing till the last moment to throw away such wonderful and beautiful things. The raw traveller not only sees something mysterious, picturesque, or classical in every object that meets his eye after passing the frontier, from the children's toys to palaces and general festivals, but is apt to discern wisdom and solemnity in everything that is said to him, from the greeting of the landlord to the speculations of the politician. If not guarded against, this natural tendency will more or less vitiate the observer's first impressions, and introduce something of the ludicrous into his record of them.

From the consideration of the requisites for observation in the traveller himself, we now proceed to indicate what he is to observe, in order to inform himself of foreign Morals and Manners.

Part Two: What To Observe

Nous nous en tiendrons aux moeurs, aux habitudes extérieures
dont se forme, pour les differentes classes de la société, une
sorte de physionomie morale, où se retracent les moeurs privées.

De Jouy

It is a perpetual wonder to an inexperienced person that the students of particular classes of facts can learn so much as they do from a single branch of inquiry. Tell an uninformed man of the daily results of the study of Fossil Remains, and he will ask how the student can possibly know what was done in the world ages before man was created. It will astonish a thoughtless man to hear the statements about the condition of the English nation which are warranted by the single study of the administration of the Poor Laws, since their origin. Some physiognomists fix their attention on a single feature of the human face, and can pretty accurately interpret the general character of the mind from it: and I believe every portrait painter trusts mainly to one feature for the fidelity of his likenesses, and bestows more study and care on that one than on any other.

A good many features compose the physiognomy of a nation; and scarcely any traveller is qualified to study them all. The same man is rarely enlightened enough to make investigation at once into the religion of a people, into its general moral notions, its domestic and economical state, its political condition, and the facts of its progress;--all which are necessary to a full understanding of its morals and manners. Few have even attempted an inquiry of this extent. The worst of it is that few dream of undertaking the study of any one feature of society at all. We should by this time have been rich in the knowledge of nations if each intelligent traveller had endeavored to report of any one department of moral inquiry, however narrow; but, instead of this, the observations offered to us are almost purely desultory. The traveller hears and notes what this and that and the other person says. If three or four agree in their statements on any point, he remains unaware of a doubt, and the matter is settled. If they differ, he is perplexed, does not know whom to believe, and decides, probably, in accordance with prepossessions of his own. The case is almost equally bad, either way. He will hear only one side of every question if he sees only one class of persons,--like the English in America, for instance, who go commonly with letters of introduction from merchants at home to merchants in the maritime cities, and hear nothing but federal politics, and see nothing but aristocratic manners. They come home with notions which they suppose to be indisputable about the great Bank question, the state of parties, and the relations of the General and State governments; and with words in their mouths of whose objectionable character they are unaware,--about the common people, mob government, the encroachment of the poor upon the rich, and so on. Such partial intercourse is fatal to the observations of a traveller; but it is less perplexing and painful at the time than the better process of going from one set of people to another, and hearing what all have to say. No traveller in the United States can learn much of the country without conversing equally with farmers and merchants, with artizans and statesmen, with villagers and planters; but, while discharging this duty, he will be so bewildered with the contrariety of statements and convictions, that he will often shut his note-book in a state of skepticism as to whether there be any truth at all shining steadily behind all this tempest of opinions. Thus it is with the stranger who traverses the streets of Warsaw, and is trusted with the groans of some of the outraged mourners who linger in its dwellings; and then goes to St. Petersburg, and is presented with evidences of the enlightenment of the Czar, of his humanity, his paternal affection for his subjects, and his general superiority to his age. At Warsaw the traveller called him a miscreant; at Petersburg he is required to pronounce him a philanthropist. Such must be the uncertainty of judgment when it is based upon the testimony of individuals. To arrive at the facts of the condition of a people through the discourse of individuals, is a hopeless enterprise. The plain truth is--it is beginning at the wrong end.

The grand secret of wise inquiry into Morals and Manners is to begin with the study of *things*, using the *discourse of persons* as a commentary upon them.

Though the facts sought by travellers relate to Persons, they may most readily be learned from Things. The eloquence of Institutions and Records, in which the action of the nation is embodied and perpetuated, is more comprehensive and more faithful than that of any variety of individual voices. The voice of a whole people goes up in the silent workings of an institution; the condition of the masses is reflected from the surface of a record. The Institutions of a nation,--political, religious, or social,--put evidence into the observer's hands as to its capabilities and wants which the study of individuals could not yield in the course of a lifetime. The Records of any society, be they what they may, whether architectural remains, epitaphs, civic registers, national music, or any other of the thousand manifestations of the common mind which may be found among every people, afford more information on Morals in a day than converse with individuals in a year. Thus also must Manners be judged of, since there never was a society yet, not even a nunnery or a Moravian settlement, which did not include a variety of manners. General indications must be looked for, instead of generalizations being framed from the manners of individuals. In cities, do social meetings abound? and what are their purposes and character? Are they most religious, political, or festive? If religious, have they more the character of Passion Week at Rome, or of a camp-meeting in Ohio? If political, do the people meet on wide plains to worship the Sun of the Celestial Empire, as in China; or in town-halls, to remonstrate with their representatives, as in England; or in secret places, to spring mines under the thrones of their rulers, as in Spain? If festive, are they most like an Italian carnival, where everybody laughs; or an Egyptian holiday, when all eyes are solemnly fixed on the whirling Dervishes? Are women there? In what proportions, and under what law of liberty? What are the public amusements? There is an intelligible difference between the opera at Milan, and the theatre at Paris, and a bull-fight at Madrid, and a fair at Leipzig, and a review at St. Petersburg.--In country towns, how is the imitation of the metropolis carried on? Do the provincials emulate most in show, in science, or in the fine arts?--In the villages, what are the popular amusements? Do the people meet to drink or to read, to discuss, or play games, or dance? What are the public houses like? Do the people eat fruit and tell stories? or drink ale and talk politics or call for tea and saunter about? or coffee and play dominoes? or lemonade and laugh at Punch? Do they crowd within four walls, or gather under the elm, or spread themselves abroad over the cricket-field or the yellow sands?--There is as wide a difference among the humbler classes of various countries as among their superiors in rank. A Scotch burial is wholly unlike the ceremonies of the funeral pile among the Cingalese; and an interment in the Greek church little resembles either. A conclave of White Boys in Mayo, assembled in a mud hovel on a heath, to pledge one another to their dreadful oath, is widely different from a similar conclave of Swiss insurgents, met in a pine wood on a steep, on the same kind of errand: and both are as little like as may be to the heroes of the last revolution in Paris, or to the companies of Covenanters that were wont to meet, under a similar pressure of circumstances, in the defiles of the Scottish mountains.--In the manners of all classes, from the highest to the lowest, are forms of manners enforced in action, or dismissed in words? Is there barbarous freedom in the lower, while there is formality in the higher ranks, as in newly settled countries? or have all grown up together to that period of refined civilization when ease has superseded alike the freedom of the Australian peasantry, and the etiquette of the court of Ava?--What are the manners of professional men of the society, from the eminent lawyer or physician of the metropolis down to the village barber? The manners of the great body of the professional men must indicate much of the requisitions of the society they serve.--So, also, must every circumstance connected with the service of society: its character, whether slavish or free, abject or prosperous, comprehensive or narrow in its uses, must testify to the desires and habits, and therefore to the manners of a community, better than the conversation or deportment of any individual in the society can do. A traveller who bears all this in mind can hardly go wrong. Everything that he looks upon will instruct him, from an aqueduct to a punch-bowl, from a penitentiary to an aviary, from the apparatus of a university to the furniture of an alehouse or a nursery. When it was found that the chiefs of the Red men could not be impressed with any notion of the civilization of the Whites by all that many white men could say, they were brought into the cities of the Whites. The exhibition of a ship was enough for some. The warriors of the prairies were too proud to utter their astonishment,--too noble to hint, even to one another, their fear; but the perspiration stood on their brows as they dumbly gazed, and no word of war passed their lips from that hour. Another, who could listen with calmness to the tales of boastful traders in the wilderness, was moved from his apathy by seeing a workman in a glasshouse put a handle upon a pitcher. He was transported out of his silence and reserve: he seized and grasped the hand of the workman, crying out that it was now plain that he had had intercourse with the Great Spirit. By the evidence of things these Indians had learned more of the manners of the Whites than had ever been taught them by speech.--Which of us would not learn more of the manners of the Pompeians by a morning's walk among the relics of their abodes and public halls than by many a nightly conference with certain of their ghosts?

The usual scholastic division of Morals is into personal, domestic, and social or political morals. The three kinds are, however, so apt to run into one another,--so practically inseparable,--that the traveller will find the distinction less useful to him than some others which he can either originate or adopt.

It appears to me that the Morals and Manners of a nation may be included in the following departments of inquiry--the Religion of the people; their prevalent Moral Notions; their Domestic State; their Idea of Liberty; and their Progress, actual or in prospect.

Chapter 1: Religion

Dieu nous a dit, Peuples, je vous attends.

De Beranger

Of religion, in its widest sense, (the sense in which the traveller must recognize it,) there are three kinds; not in all cases minutely distinguishable, but bearing different general impress; viz. the Licentious, the Ascetic, and the Moderate. These kinds are not divided from each other by the boundaries of sects. We cannot say that pagan religions come under one head, and Mahomedanism under another, and Christianity under a third. The difference lies not in creeds, but in spirit. Many pagans have been as moderate as any Christians; many Christians as licentious as any pagans; many Mahomedans as licentious, and many as ascetic, as any pagans or Christians. The truer distinction seems to be that the licentious religions of the world worship unspiritualized nature,--material objects and their movements, and the primitive passions of man: that the ascetic despises nature, and worships its artificial restraints: and that the moderate worships spiritualized nature,--God in his works, both in the material universe and in the disciplined human mind, with its regulated affections.

The Licentious religion is always a ritual one. Its gods are natural phenomena and human passions personified; and, when once the power of doing good or harm is attributed to them, the idea of propitiation enters, and a ritual worship begins. Earthquakes, inundations, the chase, love, revenge,--all these agents of evil and good are to be propitiated, and sacrifices and prayers are to be offered to them; in these rites alone religious acts are supposed to be performed. This, however modified, is a low state of religious sentiment. It may show itself among the Hindoos dipping in the Ganges, or among Christians who accept absolution in its grossest sense. In either case its tendency is to render the worshipper satisfied with a low moral state, and to perpetuate his taste for selfish indulgence.

The Ascetic religions are ritual also. The Pharisees of old need but be cited

47

to show why; and there is a set of people in the Society Islands now who seem to be spiritually descended from the ascetic priests of Judaism. The inhabitants of the Society Islands are excluded from many innocent privileges and natural pleasures by the Tabu; and the Pharisees in just the same manner laid burdens upon men's shoulders too heavy to be borne, ordaining irksome ceremonies to be proofs of holiness, and extravagant self-denial to be required by devotion. Spiritual license has always kept pace with this extravagance of self-denial. Spiritual vices,--pride, vanity, and hypocrisy,--are as fatal to high morals under this state of religious sentiment as sensual indulgence under the other: and it does not matter much to the moral welfare of the people sunk in it, whether they exist under a profession of Christianity, or of Mahomedanism, or of paganism. The morals of those people are low who engage themselves to serve God by a slothful life in monastic celibacy, no less than those of the Fakîrs, who let their nails grow through the backs of their hands, or those of the wretched mothers in the islands of the Pacific, who strangle their infants, and cast them at the feet of their grinning idol.

The Moderate is the least of a ritual religion of the three, and drops such rites as it has in proportion to its advance towards purity. Religion in its purity is not a pursuit, but a temper; and its expression is not by sacrifices, by prayers in the corners of the streets, by fasts or public exhibitions. The highest manifestations of this order of religion are found in Christian countries; though in others there are individuals, and even orders of men, who understand that the orderly enjoyment of all blessings that Providence has bestowed, and the regulated workings of all human affections, are the truest homage to the Maker of all. As there are Christians whose reliance is upon their ritual worship, and who enter upon a monastic life, so there are Mahomedans and pagans whose high religious aim is self-perfection, sought through the free but disciplined exercise of their whole nature.

The dependence of morals upon the character of the religion is clear. It is clear that among a people whose gods are supposed to be licentious, whose priests are licentious, and where worship is associated with the indulgence of the passions, political and domestic morals must be very low. What purity can be expected of a people whose women are demanded in turn for the obscene service of the Buddhist temple; and what humanity from the inhabitants of districts whose dwellings are necessarily closed against the multitudes flocking to the festivals of Juggernaut,--multitudes from amidst which thousands annually drop down dead, so that their skeletons strew the road to the abominable temple?--Where asceticism is the character of the religion, the natural and irrepressible exercise of human affections becomes licentiousness, so called; and, of consequence, it soon becomes licentiousness in fact, according to the general rule that a bad name changes that to which it is affixed into a bad quality.--Hannah and Philip grew up in a Moravian settlement; and, Moravians as they were, they loved. The days came when the destiny of each was decided by lot. It was scarcely possible that they should draw a lot to marry each other; yet both secretly hoped to the last. Philip drew a missionary lot, and Hannah another husband. They were allowed to shake hands once before parting. "Good-bye, Hannah!" "Good-bye, Philip!" was all that was said. If Hannah had gone off with Philip, it would have been called a profligate act; and, if they were sound Moravians, it would in fact have been so: whereas, in a community of really high morals, the profligacy would have been seen to lie in Hannah's marrying a man she did not love.

To proceed with the dependence of the morals on the character of the religion,--it is clear that in proportion as any religion encourages licentiousness, either positively or negatively,--encourages, that is to say, the excess of the passions, might will have the victory over right; the weak will succumb to the strong; and thus the condition of the poorer classes depends on the character of the religion of their country. In proportion as the religion tends to licentiousness, will the poorer classes be liable to slavery. In proportion as the religion tends to asceticism, will be the amount (other things being equal) of the hardship and want which they must sustain. In proportion as the religion approximates to the moderate, (the use without the abuse of means of enjoyment,) will the poorer classes rise to a condition of freedom and comfort.

The character of the religion serves, in like manner, as an index to that of the government. A licentious religion cannot be adopted by a people who are so moderate in their passions as to be able to govern themselves. One would not look for a display of meats offered to idols in the Capitol of the American Congress. An ascetic religion, too, inflicts personal and mutual wrongs which could never be endured among a people who agree to govern one another. There is no power which could induce such to submit to privations and sufferings which can be tolerable to none but devotees,--a small fraction of every society. Absolutism is commonly the character of the government of any country where either of these religions prevails;--a despotism more or less tempered by a variety of influences. It is the observer's business to bring the religion and the government into comparison, and to see how the latter is modified by the coexistence of the former.

The friendly, no less than the domestic and political relations of society, are dependent upon the prevailing religion. Under the licentious, the manners will be made up of the conventional and the gross. A Burmese minister was sitting on the poop of a steam-vessel when a squall came on. "I suggested to his Excellency," says Mr. Crawford, "the convenience of going below, which he long resisted, under the apprehension of committing his dignity by placing himself in a situation where persons might tread over his head; for this singular antipathy is common both to the Burmese and Siamese. The prejudice is more especially directed against the fair sex,--a pretty conclusive proof of the estimation in which they are held. His Excellency seriously demanded to know whether any woman had ever trod upon the poop; and, being assured in the negative, he consented at length to enter the cabin." The house fixed for the residence of an American missionary was not allowed to be fitted up, as it stood on ground which was higher than the king's barge as it lay in the river; and such a spectacle would not become the king's dignity. The prime minister of this same king was one day, for absence from his post at a fire, "spread out in the hot sun." He was extended on his back in the public road for some hours in the most sultry part of the day, with a heavy weight upon his chest,--the public executioners being employed to administer the punishment. Nor is the king alone authorized to perpetrate such barbarisms. A creditor is permitted to seize the wife, children, and slaves of a debtor, and bind them at his door to broil in the sun of Ava. Here we see in perfection the union of the conventional and the gross in manners; and such manners cannot be conceived to coexist with any religion of a higher character than Buddhism.

Under ascetic forms, what grossness there is will be partially concealed; but there will be no nearer an approach to simplicity than under the licentious. The religion being made still to consist much in observances, the society becomes formal in proportion as it believes itself growing pure. We must again take an extreme case for an example. The Shakers of America are as sophisticated a set of persons as can be found; with their minds, and even their public discourses, full of the one subject of their celibacy, and their intercourse with each other graduated according to strict rules of etiquette. So extreme an asceticism can never now spread in any nation to such an extent as to bear a relation to its general government: but it is observable that such societies of ascetics live under a despotism;--one of their own appointment, if the general will has not furnished them with one.

Under the moderate aspect of religion is an approximation towards simplicity of social manners alone to be found. There is as yet only a remote anticipation of it in any country in the world; only a remote anticipation of that ease of social manners which must exist there alone where the enjoyments of life are freely used without abuse. It matters not that the licentious and the ascetic parties each boast of having attained this consummation,--the one under the name of ease, and the other of simplicity. There is too much pain attendant upon grossness to justify the boast of ease; and too much effort in asceticism to admit of the grace of simplicity. It is the observer's business to mark, wherever he goes, the degree in which the one is chastened and the other relaxed, giving place to the higher form of the moderate, which, if society learns from experience, as the individual does, must finally prevail. When many individuals of a society attain that self-forgetfulness which is promoted by a high and free religious sentiment, but which is incompatible with either licentious or ascetic tendencies, the tone of manners in that society will be much raised. When, free from the grossness of self-indulgence, and from the constraint of self-denial, every one spontaneously thinks more of his neighbor than of himself, the world will witness, at last, the perfection of manners. It is clear that the high morals of which such refined manners will be the expression, must greatly depend on the exaltation of the religious sentiment from which they emanate.

The traveller may possibly object the difficulty of classing societies by their religious tendencies, and ask whether minds of every sort are not to be found in all numerous assemblages of persons. This is true: but yet there is a prevailing religious sentiment in all communities. Religious, like other sentiment, is modified by the strong general influences under which each society lives; and in it, as in other kinds, there will be general resemblance, with particular differences under it. It is well known that even sects, exclusive in their opinions and straitened by forms, differ in different countries almost as much as if there were no common bond. Not only is episcopacy not the same religion among born East Indians as in England, but the Quakers of the United States, though like the English in doctrine and in manners, are easily distinguishable from them in religious sentiment: and even the Jews, who might be expected to be the same all over the world, differ in Russia, Persia, and Great Britain as much as if a spirit of division had been sent among them. They not only appear here in furs, there in cotton or silk, and elsewhere in broadcloth; but the hearts they bear beneath the garments, the thoughts that stir under the cap, the turban, and the hat, are modified in their action as the skies under which they move are in aspect. They are strongly tinctured with the national sentiment of Russia, Persia, and England; and if the fond dream of some of them (in which, by the way, large numbers of their body have ceased to sympathize,) could come true, and they should ever be brought together within their ancient borders, they would find that their religion, so unique in its fixedness, though one in word, is many in spirit.--Much more easy is the assimilation between different forms of Christianity, and between Christianity and an elevated natural religion: and the search can never therefore be in vain for a pervading religious sentiment among the various religious institutions of any and every people.

It is, of course, more difficult to discover this religious sentiment among a nation enlightened enough to be divided in theological matters, than among a rude people who regulate their devotions by the bidding of a single order of priests. The African traveller, passing up the Niger, sees at a glance what all the worshippers on the banks feel, and must feel, towards the deities to whom their temples are erected. A rude shed, with a doll,--an image of deformity,-- perched on a stand, and supposed to be enjoying the fumes of the cooking going on before his face;--a place of worship like this, in its character of the habitation of a deity, and of a sensual deity, leaves no doubt as to what the religious sentiment of a country must be where there is no dissent from such a worship. In such a society there are absolutely none to feel that their deep palm groves are a nobler temple than human hands can rear. There are none who see that it is by a large divine benignity that all the living creatures of that region are made happy in their rank seclusion. There is no feeling of gratitude in the minds of those who see the myriads of gay butterflies that flit in the glare of noon, and the river-horse which bathes in the shady places of the mysterious great stream. There a god is seen only in his temple, and there is nothing known of any works of his. That he is great, is learned only through the word of his priests, who say that yams are too common a food for him, and that nothing less than hippopotamus' flesh must be cooked beneath his shrine. That he is good is an idea which has not yet entered any mind.--In other places, the religious sentiment is almost equally unquestionable; as when every man in Cairo is seen in his turn to put on the dress of pilgrimage, and direct his steps to Mount Arafat. Here the sentiment is of a higher order, but equally evident and uniform.--A further advance, with somewhat less uniformity of sentiment, is found among the followers of the Greek church in a Russian province. The peasants there make a great point of having time for their devotions; and those who have the wherewithal to offer some showy present at a shrine are complacent. They make the sign of the cross, and have therein done their whole duty: and if some speculative worshipper of the Virgin with Three Hands is not satisfied about the way in which his patroness came by her third hand, he keeps his doubts to himself when he tells his sins to his confessor.--A still further advance, with an increased diversity, may be met with among the simple Vaudois, the general characteristics of whose faith are alike, but who entertain it, some more in the spirit of fear, others more in the spirit of love. The prevailing sentiment among them is of the ascetic character, as the stranger may perceive, who sees the peasantry marching in serene gravity to their plain places of worship on the mountain pinnacle, or under the shelter yielded by a clump of black pines amidst a waste of snow: but here the clergy are more guides than dictators; and not a few may be found who doubt their opinions, and find matter for thoughtless delight, rather than religious awe, when they follow the echoes from steep to steep, and watch for the gleams of the summer lightning playing among the defiles.--The diversity grows more striking as civilization advances; but it has not yet become perplexing in the most enlightened nations in the world. In England, in France, in America, there is a distinct religious sentiment: in England, where there is every variety of dissent from the established faith; in America, where there is every variety of opinion, and no establishment at all; and in France, now in that state which most baffles observation,--a state of transition from an exaggerated superstition to a religious faith which is being groped for, but is not yet found. Even in this uncertain state, no one can confound the religious sentiment of New England and of France; and an observation of their places of worship will indicate their differences. In New England, the populous towns have their churches in the midst, spacious and conspicuous,-- not exhibiting any of the signs of antique origin which are impressed on those of Europe, and to be accounted for only by the immediate religious tastes of the people. In new settlements, the church rises side by side with the house of entertainment, and is obviously considered one of the necessaries of social life. The first thing to be learned about a fresh inhabitant is, how he stands disposed towards the church, whatever may be its denomination. In France, such of the old churches as are still used for their ancient purpose, bespeak a ritual religion, and therefore a religion light and gay in its spirit; all religions being so which cast responsibility into outward observances, especially where the outward observances are not of a very burdensome character. If nuns in their cloister, and Jews in their synagogues, have been characterized by the lightness of their religious spirit, well may the Catholics of an enlightened country be so, discarding the grossest and most burdensome of their rites, and retaining the ritual principle. The searchers after a new faith in France must increase by millions before they can change the character of the religious sentiment of the country; and perhaps before that which is now gross can be elevated into what is genial, and before a mixture of levity and fear can be changed into the cheerful earnestness of a moderate or truly catholic religious conviction, the ancient churches of France may be standing in ruins,--objects for the research of the antiquary.

The rule of examining things before persons must be observed in ascertaining the religious sentiment of any country. A stranger in England might interrogate everybody he saw, and be little wiser at the end of a year. He might meet a fanatic one day, an indifferent person the next, and a calmly convinced one the third: he might go from a Churchman to a Jew; from a Jew to a Quaker; from a Quaker to a Catholic; and every day be farther from understanding the prevailing religious sentiment of the country. A much shorter and surer method is, to examine the Places of Worship, the condition of the Clergy, the Popular Superstitions, the observance of Holy Days, and some other particulars of the kind.

    *   *   *   *   *

First, for the Churches. There is that about all places of worship which may tell nearly as plain a tale as the carved idols, with messes of rice before them, in Hindoo temples; or as the human bones hung round the hut of an African god. The proportion and resemblance of modern places of worship to those which were built in dark times of superstition; the suitability or incongruity of all that is of late introduction into their furniture and worship with what had its origin in those dim ages;--such circumstances as these cannot but indicate whether the common religious sentiment is as nearly as possible the same as in centuries past, or whether it is approximating, slowly or rapidly, towards the ascetic or the moderate.

There is evidence in the very forms of churches. The early Christian churches were in the basilica form,--bearing a resemblance to the Roman courts of justice. This is supposed to have arisen from the churches being, in fact, the courts of spiritual justice, where penance was awarded by the priest to the guilty, and absolution granted to the penitent. From imitation, the Christian churches of all Europe for centuries bore this form; and even some built since the Reformation preserve it. But they have something of their own which serves as a record of their own times. The history of the Crusades does not present a more vivid picture of feudal society than shines out from the nooks of our own cathedrals. The spirit of monachism is as distinguishable as if the cowled ghosts of the victims were actually seen flitting along the aisles. What say the chantries ranged along the sides? There perpetual prayers were to be kept up for the prosperity of a wealthy family and its retainers in life, and for their welfare after death. What says the chapter-house? There the powerful members of the church hierarchy were wont to assemble, to use and confirm their rule. What say the cloisters? Under their shelter did the monks go to and fro in life; and in the plot of ground enclosed by these somber passages were they laid in death. What says the Ladye chapel? What say the niches with their stone basins? They tell of the intercessory character of the sentiment, and of the ritual character of the worship of the times when they were set up. The handful of worshippers here collected from among the tens of thousands of a cathedral town also testify to the fact that such establishments could not be originated now, and are no longer in harmony with the spirit of the multitude.--The contrast of the most modern sacred buildings tells as plain a tale:--the red-brick meeting-house of the Friends; the stone chapel of the less rigid dissenters, standing back from the noise of the busy street; the aristocratic chapel nestling amidst the shades of the nobleman's park; and the village church in the meadow, with its neighboring parsonage. These all tell of a diversity of opinion; but also of something else. The more ancient buildings are scantily attended; the more modern are thronged;--and indeed, if they had not been wanted by numbers, they would not have been built. This speaks the decline of a ritual religion, and the preference of one which is more exclusively spiritual in its action.

In Scotland the kirks look exactly suitable to the population which throngs towards them, with sober dress and gait, and countenances of solemnity. These edifices stand in severe simplicity, whether on the green shore of a lake, or in the narrow street of a town; and asceticism is marked on every stone of the walls, and every article of their decorations.

No one who has travelled in Ireland can forget the aspect of its places of worship,--the lowly Catholic chapels, with their beggarly ornaments of lace and crucifixes, placed in the midst of villages, the whole of whose inhabitants crowd within those four walls; and a little way off, in a field, or on an eminence by the road side, the Protestant church, one end in ruins, and with ample harborage for the owl, while the rest is encompassed with nettles and thorns, and the mossy grave-stones are half hidden by rank grass. In a country where the sun rises upon contrasts like these, it is clear in what direction the religious sentiment of the people is indulged.

What the stranger may thus learn in our own country, we may learn in his, whatever it be. The large plain churches of Massachusetts, their democratic benches (in the absence of aristocratic pews) silently filled for long hours of a Sabbath, as still as a summer noon, by hundreds and thousands who restore the tones of their pilgrim ancestors in their hymn-singing, and seem to carry about their likeness in their faces, cannot fail to instruct the observer.--Then there is the mosque at Cairo, with its great tank or fountain of ablution in the midst; and its broad pavement spread out for men of every degree to kneel on together; its doors standing wide from sunrise to sunset, for the admission of all but women and strangers; its outside galleries, from which the summons to prayer is sounded;--these things testify to the ritual character of the worship, and to the low type of the morals of a faith which despises women and strangers, giving privileges to the strong from which the weak are excluded.-- Then there is the Buddhist temple, rearing its tapering form in a recess of the hills, with its colossal stone figures guarding the entrance, and others sanctifying the interior,--all eloquently explaining that physical force is worshipped here: its images of saints show that the intercessory superstition exists; and the drum and gong, employed to awaken the attention of the gods, can leave little danger of misapprehension to the observer. There are lanterns continually burning, and consecrated water, sanctified to the cure of diseased eyes.--Such places of worship tell a very plain tale; while there is not perhaps a church on earth which does not convey one that is far from obscure.

The traveller must diligently visit the temples of nations; he must mark their locality, whether placed among men's dwellings or apart from them; their number, whether multiplied by diversity of theological opinion; and their aspect, whether they are designed for the service of a ritual or a spiritual religion. Thus he may, at the same time, ascertain the character of the most prominent form of religion, and that of the dissent from it; which must always illustrate each other.

*　　*　　*　　*　　*

Next to the Churches comes the consideration of the Clergy. The clergy are usually the secondary potentates of a young country. In a young country, physical force, and that which comes to represent it, is the first great power; and knowledge is the next. The clergy are the first learned men of every nation; and when the streams of knowledge are only just issuing from the fountain, and the key is in the hands of the clergy, they enjoy, rightly and unavoidably, a high degree of consequence. Knowledge spreads abroad; and it is as impossible for man to dam it up as for the fool to stop the Danube by filling the narrow channel at its source with his great boots,--crying out the while, "How the people will wonder when the Danube does not come!" As knowledge becomes diffused, the consequence of the clergy declines. If that consequence is to be preserved, it must be by their attaining the same superiority in morals which they once held in intellect. Where the clergy are now a cherished class, it is, in fact, on the supposition of this moral superiority,--a claim for whose justification it would be unreasonable to look, and for the forfeiture of which the clergy should be less blamed than those who expect that, in virtue of a profession, any class of men should be better than others. Moral excellence has no regard to classes and professions; and religion, being not a pursuit but a temper, cannot, in fact, be professionally cultivated with personal advantage. It will be for the traveller to note whether this is more or less understood where he travels; whether the clergy are viewed with indifference as mere professional men; or whether they are reverenced for their supposed holiness; or for their real superiority in learning; or whether the case wears the lowest aspect of all--when the clergy are merely the jugglers and puppet-masters of the multitude. A patient consideration of this will lead to a pretty safe conclusion as to the progress the people have made in knowledge, and the spiritual freedom which it brings;--a freedom which is at once a virtue and a cause of virtue.

The observer must note what the clergy themselves consider their function to be;--whether to guide individual minds; or to cultivate theological and other studies, in order to place their results at the disposal of the minds with which they have to deal; or to express in worship the feelings of those minds; or to influence the social institutions by which the minds of the people are modified; or to do any other of the many things which the priests of different countries, and ages, and faiths, have in turn included in their function. He will note whether they are most like the tyrannical Brahmins, who at one stroke--

by declaring the institution of Caste to be of divine authority--obtained boundless control over a thousand generations, subjecting all intellects and all hands to a routine which could be easily superintended by the forty thousand of the favored priestly race; or whether they are like the Christian clergy of the dark ages, a part of whose duty it was to learn the deepest secrets of the proudest and lowliest,--thus obtaining the means of bringing to pass what events they wished, both in public and private life;--or whether they are like such students as have been known in the theological world,--men who have not crossed the threshold of their libraries for eighteen years, and who are satisfied with their lives, if they have been able to elevate Biblical science, and to throw any new light on sacred history;--or whether they are like the American clergy of the present day, whose exertions are directed towards the art of preaching;--or whether they are like the ministers of the Established Church in England, who are politically represented, and large numbers of whom employ their influence for political purposes. Each of these kinds of clergy must be yielded by a particular state of society, and could not belong to any other. The Hindoos must be in a low degree of civilization, and sunk in a deadly superstition, or they would tolerate no Brahmins. The people of four centuries ago must have depended solely upon their priests for knowledge and direction, or they would not have submitted to their inquisitorial practices. Germany must have advanced far in her appreciation of philosophical and critical research in theology, or she would not have such devoted students as she can boast of. The Americans cannot have attained to any high practice of spiritual liberty, or they could not follow preaching so zealously as they do. The English cannot have fully understood, or taken to heart the principles of the Reformation, which have so long been their theme of eulogy, or they would not foster a political hierarchy within the bosom of their church.

As the studies of the clergy lie in the past, as the days of their strongest influence are behind, and as the religious feelings of men have hitherto reposed on the antique, and are but just beginning to point towards the future, it is natural, it is unavoidable, that the clergy should retard rather than aid the progress of society. A disposition to assist in the improvement of institutions is what ought not to be looked for from any priestly class; and, if looked for, it will not be found. Such a mode of operation must appear to them suicidal. But much may be learned by comparing the degree of clerical resistance to progression with the proportion of favor in which the clergy are held by the people. Where that resistance is greatest, and a clerical life is one of peculiar worldly ease, the state of morals and manners must be low. Where that resistance is least, where any social improvement whatever is found to originate with the clergy, and where they bear a just share of toil, the condition of morals and manners cannot be very much depressed. Where there is an undue partition of labor and its rewards among the clergy themselves,--where some do the work and others reap the recompense,--the fair inference is that morals and manners are in a state of transition. Such a position of affairs cannot be a permanent one; and the observer may be assured that the morals and manners of the people are about to be better than they have been.--The characteristics of the clergy will indicate, or at least direct attention to, the characteristics of dissent: and any extensive form of dissent is no other than the most recent exposition of the latest condition of morals among a large, active, and influential portion of the people. A foreign traveller in Germany, in Luther's time, could learn but little of the moral state of that empire, if he shut his eyes to the philosophy and the deeds of the reformers. If he saw nothing in the train of nuns winding down into the valleys from their now unconsecrated convent on the steep; if the tidings of the marriage of Catherine de Boria came to him like any other wedding news; if he did not mark the subdued triumph in family faces when the Book--Luther's Bible--was brought out for the daily lecture; if the decrees of Worms seemed to him like the common orders of the church, and the leveling of altars and unroofing of crypts was in his eyes but masons' work, he was not qualified to observe the people of Germany, and had no more title to report of them than if he had never left home. Thus it is now, in less extreme cases. The traveller in Spain knows little of the Spaniards unless he is aware of the theological studies, and the worship without forms, which are carried on in private by those who are keeping alive the fires of liberty in that priest and tyrant-ridden country. The foreigner in England will carry away but a partial knowledge of the religious sentiment of the people if he enters only the cathedrals of cities and the steepled churches in the villages, passing by the square meeting-houses in the manufacturing towns, and hearing nothing of the conferences, the assemblies, and the missionary enterprises of the dissenters. The same may be said of observation in every country enlightened enough to have shaken off its subservience to an unquestioned and irresponsible priesthood: that is, of every country advanced enough to maintain dissent.

The expressions of established forms of prayer convey more information as to the state of the clergy than of the people; since these expressions are furnished by the clergy, and continue to be prompted by them, while the people have no means of dismissing or changing the words of their framed prayers for long after the words may have ceased to represent the feeling. The traveller will receive such objectionable expressions as he may hear, not as indications of the then present sentiments of the crowd of worshippers, but rather as evidencing the disinclination of the clergy to change. It would be hard, for instance, to impute to Moslem worshippers in general the formation of such desires as are uttered by the school-boys of Cairo at the close of their daily attendance. "O God! destroy the infidels and polytheists, thine enemies, the enemies of the religion! O God! make their children orphans, and defile their abodes, and cause their feet to slip, and give them and their families, and their households, and their women, and their children, and their relations by marriage, and their brothers, and their friends, and their possessions, and their race, and their wealth, and their lands, as booty to the Moslems! O Lord of all creatures!"--It would be unjust to impute a horror of "sudden death" to all who use the words of prayer against it which are found in the Litany of the Church of England. Sudden death deserved to be classed among the most deadly evils when the Litany was framed,--in the days of the viaticum; but now it would be unjust to a multitude of worshippers who use the Litany to suppose that they are afraid to commit themselves to the hands of their Father without a passport from a priest; and that they are not willing to die in the way which pleases God,--some rather preferring, probably, a mode which will save those who are nearest and dearest to them the anguish of suspense, or of witnessing hopeless decline. In all antique forms of devotion there must be expressions which are inconsistent with the philosophy and the tastes of the time; and these are to be regarded therefore as no indications of such philosophy and taste, but as an evidence, more or less distinct, of the condition of the clergy in enlightenment and temper.

*   *   *   *   *

The splendid topic of human Superstitions can be only just touched upon here. In this boundless field, strewn with all the blossoms of all philosophy, the human observer may wander forever. He can never have done culling the evidence that it presents, or enjoying the promise which it yields. All that we can now do is just to suggest that as the superstitions of all nations are the embodiment of their idealized convictions, the state of religious sentiment may be learned from them almost without danger of mistake.

No society is without its superstitions, any more than it is without its convictions and its imaginations. Even under the moderate form of religion, there is room for superstition; and the ascetic, which glories in having put away the superstitions of the licentious forms, has superstitions of its own.-- The followers of an ascetic religion have more or less belief in judgments,--in retributive evils, arbitrarily inflicted. Among them may be gathered a harvest of tales of divine interference,--from the bee stinging the tip of the swearer's tongue to the sudden death of false witnesses. Among them do superstitions about times and seasons flourish, even to the forgetfulness that the Sabbath is made for man, and not man for the Sabbath. Some ascetics have faith in the lot,--like the Moravians in ordering marriage, or Wesley in opening his Bible to light upon texts. Others believe in warnings of evil; and most dread the commission of ritual fully as much as of moral sins. To play even a hymn tune on the piano on Sundays is an offence in the Highlands of Scotland; and to miss prayers is a matter of penance in a convent. The superstitions of the ascetic are scarcely fewer or more moderate than those of the licentious form of religion; the chief difference between the two lies in the spirit from which they emanate. The superstitions of the ascetic arise from the spirit of fear; those of the heathen arise perhaps equally from the spirit of love and the spirit of fear.

It seems as if the portents which present themselves to ascetic minds must necessarily be of evil, since the only good which their imaginations admit is supposed to be secured by grace, and by acts of service or self-denial. To the Fakîr, to the Shaker, to the nun, no good remains over and above what has been long claimed, while punishment may follow any breach of observance. On the other hand, before one who makes himself gods of the movements of inanimate nature and human passions, the two worlds of evil and good lie open, and he is perpetually on the watch for messengers from both. The poor pagan looks for tokens of his gods being pleased or angry; of their intentions of giving him a good or a bad harvest; or of their sending him a rich present or afflicting him with a bereavement. Whatever he wants to know, he seeks for in portents;--whether he shall live again,--whether his departed friends think of him,--whether his child shall be fortunate or wretched,--whether his enemy or he shall prevail. It is open to the traveller's observation whether these superstitions are of a generous or selfish kind,--whether they elevate the mind with hope, or depress it with fear,--whether they nourish the faith of the spirit, or extort merely the service of the lip and hand.

The Swiss herdsmen believe that the three deliverers (the founders of the Helvetic Confederacy) sleep calmly in a cave near the Lake of Lucerne; and that, whenever their country is in her utmost need, they will come forth in their antique garb, and assuredly save her. This is a superstition full of veneration and hope.--When the Arabs see a falling star, they believe it to be a dart thrown by God at a wanderer of the race of the genii, and they exclaim, "May God transfix the enemy of the faith!" Here we find in brief the spirit of their religion.--In Brazil, a bird which sings plaintively at night is listened to with intent emotion, from its being supposed to be sent with tidings from the dead to the living. The choice of a bird with a mournful instead of a lively note speaks volumes.--The three angels in white that come to give presents to good children in Germany at Christmas, come in a good spirit.--There is a superstition in China which has a world of tenderness in it. A father collects a hundred copper coins from a hundred families, and makes the metal into a lock which he hangs, as a charm, round his child's neck, believing that he locks his child to life by this connection with a hundred persons in full vigor.--But, as is natural, death is the region of the Unseen to which the larger number of portents relates. The belief of the return of the dead has been held almost universally among the nations; and their unseen life is the grand theme of speculation wherever there are men to speculate. The Norwegians lay the warrior's horse, and armor, and weapons, beside him. The Hindoos burn the widow. The Malabar Indians release caged birds on the newly-made grave, to sanction the flight of the soul. The Buccaneers (according to Penrose) concealed any large booty that fell into their hands, till they should have leisure to remove it,--murdering and burying near it any helpless wretch whom they might be able to capture, in order that his spirit might watch over the treasure, and drive from the spot all but the parties who had signed their names in a round-robin, in claim of proprietorship. The professors of many faiths resemble each other in practices of propitiation or atonement laboriously executed on behalf of the departed. Some classes of mourners act towards their dead friends in a spirit of awe; some in fear; but very many in love. The trust in the immortality of the affections is the most general feature in superstitions of this class; and it is a fact eloquent to the mind of the observer.--An only child of two poor savages died. The parents appeared inconsolable; and the father soon sank under his grief. From the moment of his death, the mother was cheerful. On being asked what had cheered her, she said she had mourned for her child's loneliness in the world of spirits: now he had his father with him, and she was happy for them both. What a divine spirit of self-sacrifice is here! but there is scarcely a superstition sincerely entertained which does not tell as plain a tale. Those which express fear indicate moral abasement, greater or less. Those which express trust and love indicate greater or less moral elevation and purity.

    *   *   *   *   *

The practice of Suicide is worth the contemplation of a traveller, as affording some clear indications as to religious sentiment. Suicide in the largest sense is here intended,--the voluntary surrender of life from any cause.

There has been a stage in the moral advancement of every nation when suicide, in one form or another, has been considered a duty; and it is impossible to foresee the time when it will cease to be so considered. It was a necessary result from the idea of honor once prevalent in the most civilized societies, when men and women destroyed themselves to avoid disgrace. The defeated warrior, the baffled statesman, the injured woman, destroyed themselves when the hope of honor was gone. In the same age, as in every succeeding one, there have been suicides who have devoted themselves for others, presenting a series of tales which may almost redeem the disgraces which darken the annals of the race.--The most illustrious of the Christian Fathers, immersed in the superstitions about the transcendent excellence of the virtue of chastity which have extinguished so many other virtues, and

61

injured the morals of society to this day, by sacrificing other principles to fanaticism on this, permitted women to kill themselves to escape from violence which left the mind in its purity, and the will in its rectitude.-- Martyrdom for the truth existed also before the venerating eyes of men,--the noblest kind of suicide: it attracted glory to itself from the faithful heart of the race; and, from its thus attracting glory, it became a means of gaining glory, and sank from being martyrdom to be a mere fanatical self-seeking. While the spirit of persecution was roaming abroad, seeking whom it might devour, there were St. Theresas roaming abroad, seeking to be devoured, from a spirit of cupidity after the crown of martyrdom.--Soldiers, in all times and circumstances, pledge themselves to the possible duty of suicide by the very act of becoming soldiers. They engage to make the first charge, and to mount a breach if called upon. And there have been found soldiers for every perilous service that has been required, throughout all wars. There have been volunteers to mount the breach, solitary men or small bands to hold narrow bridges and passes, from the first incursion of tribe upon tribe in barbarous conflict, up to the suicide of Van Speyk, whose monument is still fresh from the chisel in the Nieuw Kerk of Amsterdam. Van Speyk commanded a gun-boat which was stranded in a heavy gale, and boarded by the Belgians,--the foe. Van Speyk had sworn never to surrender his boat, and his suicide was a point of military honor. He seems to have considered the matter thus; for he prayed for pardon of his crime of self-destruction after laying his lighted cigar on the open barrel of powder which blew up the boat. The remaining suicides (except, of course, the insane,) are justified by none. Persons who shrink from suffering so far as to withdraw from their duties, and to forsake those to whom their exertions are due, are objects of contemptuous compassion in the present day, when, moral having succeeded to physical force in men's esteem, it is seen to be nobler to endure evils than to hide one's spirit from them.

Every society has its suicides, and much may be learned from their character and number, both as to the notions on morals which prevail, and the religious sentiment which animates to or controls the act. It is with the last that we now have to do.--The act of laying down life is one thing among a people who have dim and mournful anticipations of a future life, like the ancient Greeks; and quite another among those who, like the first Christians, have a clear vision of bliss and triumph in the world on which they rush. Suicide is one thing to a man who is certain of entering immediately upon purgatory; and to another whose first step is to be upon the necks of his enemies; and to a third who believes that he is to lie conscious in his grave for some thousands of years; and to a fourth who has no idea that he shall survive or revive at all. When Curtius leaped into the gulf, he probably leaped into utter darkness, other than physical; but when Guyon of Marseilles sunned himself for the last time in the balcony of the house where he was shut up with the plague-spotted body which he was to die in dissecting, he had faith that he should step out of a waxing and waning sunlight into a region which "had no need of the sun, neither of the moon, to shine in it, the glory of God being the light of it." The sick Moslem who, falling behind his troop, and fearing to lie unburied, scoops his grave and lies down in it, wrapped in his grave-clothes, and covers himself up, except the face, leaving it to the winds to heap sand upon it, trembles the while at the thought of the two examining angels, who are this night to prove and perhaps torture him. The English lady who took laudanum on learning that she had a fatal disease, from fear of becoming loathsome to a husband for whom she had lived, had before her the prominent idea of reunion with him; so that life in one world presented as much of hope as in the other of despair.--Nations share in differences like these, according to the prevalent religious sentiment; and from this species of act may the sentiment be more or less correctly inferred.

Suicide is very common among a race of Africans who prefer it to slavery. They believe in a life of tropical ease and freedom after death, and rush into it so eagerly on being reduced to slavery, that the planters of Cuba refuse them in the market, knowing that after a few hours, or days, in spite of all precautions, nothing but their dead bodies will remain in the hands of their masters. The French have, of late years, abounded in suicides, while there are few or none in Ireland. The most vain and the most sympathetic part of the French multitude were found to be the classes which yielded the victims. If a young lady and her lover shot one another with pistols tied with pink ribbons, two or three suicides amidst blue and green ribbons were sure to follow the announcement of the first in the newspaper, till a sensible physician suggested that suicides should not be noticed in newspapers, or should be treated with ridicule: the advice was acted upon, and proved by the result to be sound. This profusion of self-murders could not have taken place amidst a serious belief of an immediate entrance upon purgatory, such as is held by the majority of the Irish. Only in a state of vague speculation as to another life could the future have operated as so slight a check upon the rash impulses of the present. The Irish, an impetuous race, like the French, and with a good share of vanity, of sympathy, and of sentiment, are probably deterred from throwing away life by those religious convictions and sentiments which the French once held in an equal degree, but from which they are now passing over into another state.

A single act of suicide is often indicative, negatively or positively, of a state of prevalent sentiment. A single instance of the Suttee testifies to the power of Brahmins, and the condition of Hindoo worshippers, in a way which cannot be mistaken. An American child of six years old accidentally

63

witnessed in India such a spectacle. On returning home, she told her mother she had seen hell, and was whipped for saying so,--not knowing why, for she spoke in all earnestness, and, as it seems to us, with eloquent truth.--The somewhat recent self-destruction of an estimable English officer, on the eve of a court-martial, might fully instruct a stranger on the subject of military honor in this country. This officer fell in the collision of universal and professional principles. His justice and humanity had led him to offer a kindly bearing towards an irresolute mob of rioters, in the absence of authority to act otherwise than as he did, and of all co-operation from the civil power; his military honor was placed in jeopardy, and the innocent man preferred self-destruction to meeting the risk; thus testifying that numbers here sustain an idea of honor which is at variance with that which they expect to prevail elsewhere and hereafter.--Every act of self-devotion for others, extending to death, testifies to the existence of philanthropy, and to its being regarded as an honor and a good. Every voluntary martyrdom tells a national tale as plain as that written in blood and spirit by Arnold Von Winkelried, in 1386. When the Swiss met their oppressors at the battle of Sempach, it appeared impossible for the Swiss to charge with effect, so thick was the hedge of Austrian lances. Arnold Von Winkelried cried, "I will make a lane for you! Dear companions, remember my family!" He clasped an armful of the enemy's lances, and made a sheaf of them in his body. His comrades entered the breach, and won the battle. They remembered his family, and their descendants commemorate the sacrifice to this day; thus bearing testimony to the act being a trait of the national spirit.

By observations such as these, may the religious sentiment of a people be ascertained. While making them, or struggling with the difficulties of opposing evidence, the observer has to bear in mind,--first, that the religious sentiment does everywhere exist, however low its tone, and however uncouth its expression; secondly, that personal morals must greatly depend on the low or high character of the religious sentiment; and, thirdly, that the philosophy and morals of government accord with both,--despotism of some sort being the natural rule where licentious and ascetic religions prevail; and democratic government being possible only under a moderate form of religion, where the use without the abuse of all blessings is the spirit of the religion of the majority.

Chapter 2: General Moral Notions

Une différente coutume donnera d'autres principes naturels. Cela
se voit par expérience; et s'il y en a d'ineffaçables à la coutume,
il y en a aussi de la coutume ineffaçables à la nature.

--Pascal

Next to the religion of a people, it is necessary to learn what are their
Ideas of Morals. In speaking of the popular notion of a Moral Sense, it was
mentioned that, so far from there being a general agreement on the practice of
morals, some things which are considered eminently right in one age or
country are considered eminently wrong in another; while the people of each
age or country, having grown up under common influences, think and feel
sufficiently alike to live together in a general agreement as to right and wrong.
It is the business of the traveller to ascertain what this general agreement is in
the society he visits.

In one society, spiritual attainments will be the most highly honored, as in
most religious communities. In another, the qualities attendant upon
intellectual eminence will be worshipped,--as now in countries which are the
most advanced in preparation for political freedom,--France, Germany, and
the United States. In others, the moral qualities allied to physical or extrinsic
power are chiefly venerated,--as in all uncivilized countries, and all which lie
under feudal institutions.

The lower moral qualities which belong to the last class have been
characteristics of nations. The valor of the Spartans, the love of glory of the
Romans and the French, the pride of the Spaniards,--these infantile moral
qualities have belonged to a people as distinctly as to an individual.--Those
which are in alliance with intellectual eminence are not so strikingly
characteristic of entire nations; though we praise the Athenians for their love
of letters and honor of philosophy; the Italians for their liberality towards art,
and their worship of it while a meaner glory was the fashion of the world; the
Germans for their speculative enterprise, and patience of research; and the

Americans for their reverence for intellect above military fame and the splendor of wealth.--No high spiritual qualities have ever yet characterized a nation, or even--in spite of much profession--any considerable community. Hospitality and beneficence have distinguished some religious societies: the non-resistance of Quakers, the industry of Moravians, and of several kinds of people united on the principle of community of property, may be cited: but this seems to be all. The enforced temperance, piety, and chastity of monastic societies go for nothing in this view; because, being enforced, they indicate nothing of the sentiment subsequent to the taking of the vow. The people of the United States have come the nearest to being characterized by lofty spiritual qualities. The profession with which they set out was high,--a circumstance greatly to their honor, though (as might have been expected) they have not kept up to it. They are still actuated by ambition of territory, and have not faith enough in moral force to rely upon it, as they profess to do. The Swiss, in their unshaken and singularly devoted love of freedom, seem to be spiritually distinguished above other nations: but they have no other strong characteristic of this highest class.

The truth is that, whatever may be the moral state of nations when the human world emerges hereafter from its infancy, high spiritual qualities are now matters of individual concern, as those of the intellectual class were once; and their general prevalence is a matter of prospective vision alone. Time was when the swampy earth resounded with the tramp and splash of monstrous creatures, whom there was no reason present to classify, and no language to name. Then, after a certain number of ages, the earth grew drier; palm-groves and tropical thickets flourished where Paris now stands; and the waters were collected into lakes in the regions where the armies of Napoleon were of late encamped. Then came the time when savage, animal man appeared, using his physical force like the lower animals, and taught by the experience of its deficiency that he was in possession of another kind of force. Still, for ages, the use he made of reason was to overcome the physical force of others, and to render available his own portion. On this principle, and for this object, variously modified, and more or less refined, have societies been formed to this day; though, as morals are the fruit of which intellect is the blossom, spiritualism--faith in moral power--has existed in individuals ever since the first free exercise of reason. While all nations were ravaging one another as they had opportunity, there were always parents who did not abuse their physical power over their children. In the midst of a general worship of power, birth, and wealth, the affections have wrought out in individual minds a preference of obscurity and poverty for the sake of spiritual objects. Amidst the supremacy of the worship of honor and social ease, there have always been confessors who could endure disgrace for the truth, and martyrs who could die for it.--Such individual cases have never been wanting: and, in necessary connection with this fact, there has always been a sympathy in this pure moral taste,--an appreciation which could not but help its diffusion. Thence arose the formation of communities for the fostering of holiness,--projects which, however mistaken in their methods and injurious in their consequences, have always commanded, and do still command, sympathy, from the venerableness of their origin. Not all the stories of the abuses of monastic institutions can destroy the respect of every ingenuous mind for the spiritual preferences out of which they arose. The Crusades are still holy, notwithstanding all their defilements of vain-glory, superstition, and barbarism of various kinds. The retreat of the Pilgrim Fathers to the forests of the New World silences the ridicule of the thoughtless about the extravagances of Puritanism in England.

Thus far has the race advanced; and, having thus advanced, there is reason to anticipate that the age may come when the individual worship of spiritual supremacy may expand into national; when a people may agree to govern one another with the smallest possible application of physical force; when goodness shall come to be naturally more honored than birth, wealth, or even intellect; when ambition of territory shall be given up; when all thought of war shall be over; when the pursuit of the necessaries and luxuries of external life shall be regarded as means to an end; and when the common aim of exertion shall be self and mutual perfection. It does not seem to be rash to anticipate such a state of human affairs as this, when an aspiration like the following has been received with sympathy by thousands of republicans united under a constitution of ideas. "Talent and worth are the only eternal grounds of distinction. To these the Almighty has affixed his everlasting patent of nobility; and these it is which make the bright, 'the immortal names,' to which our children may aspire, as well as others. It will be our own fault if, in our land, society as well as government is not organized on a new foundation."--"Knowledge and goodness,--these make degrees in heaven, and they must be the graduating scale of a true democracy."[F]

Meantime, it is the traveller's business to learn what is the species of Moral Sentiment which lies deepest in the hearts of the majority of the people.

*   *   *   *   *

He will find no better place of study than the Cemetery,--no more instructive teaching than Monumental Inscriptions. The brief language of the dead will teach him more than the longest discourses of the living.

He will learn what are the prevalent views of death; and when he knows what is the common view of death, he knows also what is the aspect of life to no small number;--that is, he will have penetrated into the interior of their morals.--If it should ever be fully determined that the pyramids of Egypt were designed solely as places of sepulture, they will cease to be the mute witness they have been for ages. They will tell at least that death was not regarded as the great leveler,--that kings and peasants were not to sleep side by side in death, any more than in life. How they contrast with the Moravian burial-grounds, where all are laid in rows as they happen to be brought to the grave, and where memorial is forbidden!--The dead of Constantinople are cast out from among the living in waste, stillness, and solitude. The cemeteries lie beyond the walls, where no hum from the city is heard, and where the dark cypresses overhanging the white marble tombs give an air of mourning and desolation to the scene. In contrast with these are the church-yards of English cities, whose dead thus lie in full view of the living; the school-boy trundles his hoop among them, and the news of the day is discussed above their place of rest. This fact of where the dead are laid is an important one. If out of sight, death and religion may or may not be connected in the general sentiment; if within or near the places of worship, they certainly are so connected. In the cemeteries of Persia, the ashes of the dead are ranged in niches of the walls: in Egypt we have the most striking example of affection to the body, shown in the extraordinary care to preserve it; while some half-civilized people seem to be satisfied with putting their dead out of sight, by summarily sinking them in water, or hiding them in the sand; and the Caffres throw their dead to the hyenas,--impelled to this, however, not so much by disregard of the dead, as by a superstitious fear of death taking place in their habitations, which causes them to remove the dying, and expose them in this state to beasts of prey. The burial of the dead by the road-side by some of the ancients, seems to have brought death into the closest relation with life; and when the place chosen is taken in connection with the inscriptions on the tombs,--words addressed to the wayfarer as from him who lies within,--from the pilgrim now at rest to the pilgrim still on his way, they give plain indications of the views of death and life entertained by those who placed them.

Much may be learned from the monumental inscriptions of all nations. The first epitaph is supposed to be traced back to the year of the world 2700, when the scholars of Linus, the Theban poet, bewailed their master in verses which were inscribed upon his tomb. From that day to this, wherever there have been letters, there have been epitaphs; and, where letters have been wanting, there have been symbols. Mysterious symbolic arrangements are traced in the monumental mounds in the interior of the American continent, where a race of whom we know nothing else flourished before the Red man opened his eyes upon the light. One common rule, drawn from a universal sentiment, has presided at the framing of all epitaphs for some thousands of years. "De mortuis nil nisi bonum" is the universal agreement of mourners.[G] It follows that epitaphs must everywhere indicate what is there considered good.

The observer must give his attention to this. Among a people "whose merchants are princes," the praise of the departed will be in a different strain from that which will be found among a warlike nation, or a community of agriculturists. Here one may find monumental homage to public spirit, in the form of active citizenship; there to domestic virtue as the highest honor. The glory of eminent station, of ancient family, of warlike deeds, and of courtly privileges may be conspicuously exhibited in one district; while in another the dead are honored in proportion to their contempt of human greatness, even when won by achievements; to their having lived with a sole regard "to things unseen and eternal." An inscription which breathes the pride of a noble family in telling that "all the sons were brave, and all the daughters chaste," presents a summary of the morals of the age and class to which it belongs. It tells that the supreme honor of men was to be brave, and of women to be chaste; excluding the supposition of each sharing the virtue of the other: whereas, when courage and purity shall be understood in their full signification, it will have become essential to the honor of a noble family that all the sons should be also pure, and all the daughters brave. Then bravery will signify moral rather than physical courage, and purity of mind will be considered no attribute of sex.

Even the nature of the public services commemorated, where public service is considered the highest praise, may indicate much. It is a fact of no small significance whether a man is honored after death for having made a road, or for having founded a monastery, or endowed a school; whether he introduced a new commodity, or erected a church; whether he marched adventurously in the pursuit of conquest, or fought bravely among his native mountains to guard the homes of his countrymen from aggression. The German, the French, the Swiss monuments of the present century all tell the common tale that men have lived and died: but with what various objects did they live! and in what a variety of hope and heroism did they die! All were proud of their respective differences while they lived; and, now that their contests are at an end, they afford materials of speculation to the stranger who ponders upon their tombs.

A variety, perhaps a contrariety of praise, may be found in the epitaphs of a country, a city, or a single cemetery. Where this diversity is found, it testifies to the diversity of views held, and therefore to the freedom of the prevailing religious sentiment. Everywhere, however, there is an affection and esteem for certain virtues. Disinterestedness, fidelity, and love are themes of praise everywhere. Some may have no sympathy for the deeds of the warrior, and others for the discoveries of the philosopher and the adventurer; but the honored parent, the devoted child, the philanthropic citizen, are sure of their tribute from all hearts.

Even if there were a variety of praise proportioned to the diversity of hearts and minds that utter it, the inscriptions of a cemetery cannot but breathe a spirit which must animate, more or less, the morals of the society. For instance, the cemetery of Père la Chaise utters, from end to end, one wail. It is all mourning, and no hope. Every expression of grief, from tender regret to blank despair, is to be found there; but not a hint of consolation, except from memory. All is over, and the future is vacant. A remarkable contrast to this is seen in the cemetery of Mount Auburn, Massachusetts. The religious spirit of New England is that which has hope for one of its largest elements, and which was believed by the Puritan fathers to forbid the expression of sorrow. One of those fathers made an entry in his journal, in the early days of the colony, that it had pleased God to take from him by an accident his beloved son Henry, whom he committed to the Lord's mercy;--and this was all. In a similar spirit are the epitaphs at Mount Auburn framed. There is a religious silence about the sorrows of the living, and every expression of joy, thanksgiving, and hope for the dead. One who had never heard of death, might take this for the seed-field of life; for the oratory of the happy; for the heaven of the hopeful. Parents invite their children from the grave to follow them. Children remind their parents that the term of separation will be short; and all repose their hopes together on an authority which is to them as stable and comprehensive as the blue sky which is over all.--What a contrast is here! and how eloquent as to the moral views of the respective nations! There is not a domestic attachment or social relation which is not necessarily modified, elevated, or depressed by the conviction of its being transient or immortal,--an end or means to a higher end. Though human hearts are so far alike as that there must be a hope of reunion, more or less defined and assured, in all who love, and a practical falling below the elevation of this hope in those even who enjoy the strongest assurance,--yet the moral notions of any society must be very different where the ground of hope is taken for granted, and where it is kept wholly out of sight.

*   *   *   *   *

The observer may obtain further light upon the moral ideas of a people by noting the degree of their Attachment to Kindred and Birth-place. This species of attachment is so natural, that none are absolutely without it; but it varies in degree, according as the moral taste of the people goes to enhance or to subdue it. The Swiss and the American parent both send their children abroad; but with what different feelings and views! The Swiss father dismisses his daughter to teach in a school at Paris or London, and his sons to commerce or war. He resigns himself to a hard necessity, and supports them with suggestions of the honor of virtuous independence, and of the delight of returning when it is achieved. They, in their exile, can never see a purple shade upon a mountain side, a gleaming sheet of water, or a nestling village, without a throb of the heart, and a sickening longing for home.--The New England mother, with her tribe of children around her on her hill-side farm, nourishes them with tales of the noble extent of their country,--how its boundary is ever shifting westwards, and what a wild life it is there in the forest, with the Red men for neighbors, and inexhaustible wealth in the soil, ready for the hand which shall have enterprise to work for it. She tells of one and another, but lately boys like her children, who are now judges and legislators,--founders of towns, or having counties named after them. As her young people grow up, they part off eagerly from the old farm,--one into a southern city, another into the western forest, a third to a prairie in a new territory; and the daughters marry, and go over the mountains too. The mother may have sighs to conceal, but she does conceal them; and the sons, so far from lingering,--are impatient till they are gone. Their idea of national honor,--both their patriotic and their personal ambition,--is concerned; and they welcome the hour of dispersion as the first step towards the great objects of their life. Some return to the old neighborhood to take a wife; but they do not think of passing their second childhood where they spent their first,--any more than the Greek colonists who swarmed from their narrow native districts. The settlers of the west go there, not to obtain a certain amount of personal property, but land, station, and power.--How different again are the Scotch--the people of the strongest family attachments! In the modified and elevated feudalism of clanship, pride and love of kindred constitute the animating social principle. Their clan-music is to them what the Ranz de Vaches is to the Swiss: the one echoing the harmonics of social intercourses, as the other revives the melodies of mountain life. Through the love of kindred, the love of birth-place flourishes among the Scotch. The Highland emigrants in Canada not only clasp hands when they hear played the march of their clan, but wept when they found that heather would not grow in their newly-adopted soil.

*　　*　　*　　*　　*

The traveller must talk with Old People, and see what is the character of the garrulity of age. He must talk with Children, and mark the character of the aspirations of childhood. He will thus learn what is good in the eyes of those who have passed through the society he studies, and in the hopes of those who have yet to enter upon it. Is it the aged mother's pride that her sons are all unstained in honor, and her daughters safe in happy homes? or does she boast that one is a priest, and another a peeress? Does the grandmother relate that all her descendants who are of age are "received church-members"? or that her favorite grandchild has been noticed by the emperor? Do the old men prose of a single happy love, or of exploits of gallantry? or of commercial success, or

71

of political failure? What is the section of life to which the greatest number of ancient memories cling? Is it to struggles for a prince in disguise, or to a revolutionary conflict? Is it to the removal of a social oppression, or to a season of domestic trial, or to an accession of personal consequence? Is it the having acquired an office or a title? or the having assisted in the abolition of slavery? or the having conversed with a great author? or the having received a nod from a prince, or a curtsey from a queen? or have you to listen to details of the year of the scarcity, or the season of the plague?--What are the children's minds full of? The little West Indian will not talk of choosing a profession, any more than the infant Portuguese will ask for books. One nation of children will tell of the last saint's day, and another will refer everything to the emperor. Elsewhere you will be treated with legends without end; or you will be instructed about bargains and wages; or the boys will ask you why a king's son should be king whether the people like him or not; and the girls will whisper something to you about their brother being President someday. As the minds of the young are formed, generally speaking, to an adaptation to the objects presented to them, their preference of warlike to commercial, or literary to political honor, is an eloquent circumstance: and so of their sense of greatness in any direction,--whether it be of the physical order, or the intellectual, or the spiritual.

  * * * * *

From this, the transition is natural to the study of the character of the Pride of each nation. Learn what people glory in, and you learn much of both the theory and practice of their morals. All nations, like all individuals, have pride, sooner or later, in one thing or another. It is a stage through which they have to pass in their moral progression, and out of which the most civilized have not yet advanced, nor discerned that they will have to advance, though the passion becomes moderated at each remove from barbarism. It is by no means clear that the essential absurdity of each is relieved by its dilution. Hereafter, the most modern pride of the most civilized people may appear as ridiculous in its nature as the grossest conceit of utter barbarians now appears to us; but, still, the direction taken by the general pride must show what class of objects is held in most esteem.

The Chinese have no doubt that all other countries are created for the benefit of theirs; they call their own "the central empire," as certain philosophers once called our earth the center round which everything else was to revolve. They call it the Celestial Empire, of which their ruler is the Sun: "they profess to rule barbarians by misrule, like beasts, and not like native subjects." Here we have the extreme of national pride, which must involve various moral qualities;--all the bad ones which are the consequence of ignorance, subservience to domestic despotism, and contempt of the race of man; and the good ones which are the consequence of national seclusion,--cheerful industry, social complacency, quietness, and order.--The Arab pride bears a resemblance to the Chinese, but is somewhat refined and spiritualized. The Arabs believe that the earth, "spread out like a bed," and upheld by a gigantic angel (the angel standing upon a rock, and the rock upon a bull, and the bull upon a fish, and the fish floating upon water, and the water upon darkness,)--that the earth, thus upheld, is surrounded by the Circumambient Ocean; that the inhabited part of the earth is to the rest but as a tent in the desert; and that in the very center of this inhabited part is--Mecca. Their exclusive faith makes a part of their nationality, and their insolence shows itself eminently in their devotions. Their spiritual supremacy is their strong point; and they can afford to be somewhat less outwardly contemptuous to the race at large, from the certainty they have that all will be made plain and indisputable at last, when the followers of the Prophet alone will be admitted to bliss, and the punishments of the future world will be eternal to all but wicked Mahomedans. There will be found among the Arabs, in accordance with this pride, a strong mutual fidelity; and, among the best class of believers, a real devotion and a kindly compassion towards outcasts; while, among lower orders of minds, we may expect to witness the extreme exasperation of vindictiveness, insult, and rapacity.--We may pass over the pride of caste in India, of royal race in Africa, and the wild notions of Caribbean and Esquimaux dignity, which are almost as painful to contemplate as the freaks of pride in Bedlam. There is quite enough to look upon in the most civilized parts of the earth.--The whole national character of the Spaniards might be inferred from their particularly notorious pride; the quarterings of German barons are a popular joke; the French pride of military glory is an index to the national morals of France; while, in the United States, the pride of Washington and of territory is oddly combined and contrasted. Nothing can be more indicative of the true moral state of the Americans; they hang between the past and the future, with many of the feudal prepossessions of the past, mingled with the democratic aspirations which relate to the future. The ambition and pride of territory belong to the first, and their pride in the leader of their revolution to the last: he is their personification of that moral power to which they profess allegiance. The consequences of this arbitrary union of two kinds of national pride may be foreseen. The Americans unite some of the low qualities of feudalism with some of the highest of a more equal social organization. Without the first, slavery, cupidity, and ostentation could not exist to any great extent; without the others, there could not be the splendid moral conflict which we now see going on in opposition to slavery, nor the reverence for man which is the loveliest feature of American morals and manners.

73

From the aristocratic pride of the English the stranger might draw inferences no less correct. If it is found that there is scarcely a gamekeeper or a tradesman among us who is not stiffened with prejudices about rank; that gossips can tell what noblemen pay, and which do not pay, their tradesmen's bills; that persons who have never seen a lord can furnish all information about the genealogy and intermarriages of noble families; that every class is emulating the manners of the one above it; and that democratic principles are held chiefly in the manufacturing districts, or, if in country regions, among the tenantry of landlords of liberal politics;--the moral condition of such a people lies, as it were, mapped out beneath the eye of the observer. They must be orderly, eminently industrious, munificent in their grants to rulers, and mechanically oppressive to the lowest class of the ruled; nationally complacent, while wanting in individual self-respect; reverentially inclined towards the lofty minority, and contemptuously disposed towards the lowly majority of their race; a generous devotion being advantageously mingled, however, with the select reverence, and a kindly spirit of protection with the gross contempt. Such, to the eye of an observer, are the qualities involved in English pride. Upon this moral material, everywhere diffused, should the traveller observe and reflect.

*   *   *   *   *

Man-worship is as universal a practice as that of the higher sort of religion. As men everywhere adore some supposed agents of unseen things, they are, in like manner, disposed to do homage to what is venerable when it is presented to their eyes in the actions of a living man. This man-worship is one of the most honorable and one of the most hopeful circumstances in the mind of the race. An individual here and there may scoff at the credulity of others, and profess unbelief in human virtue; but no society has ever yet wanted faith in man. Every community has its saints, its heroes, its sages,--whose tombs are visited, whose deeds are celebrated, whose words have become the rules by which men live.

Now, the moral taste of a people is nowhere more clearly shown than in its choice of idols. Of these idols there are two kinds;--those whose divinity is confirmed by the lapse of time, like Gustavus Adolphus among the Swedes, Tell in Switzerland, Henri IV. among the French, and Washington among the Americans; and those who are still living, and upon whose daily doings a multitude of eyes are fixed.

Those of the first class reign singly; their uncontested sway is over national character, as well as the affections of individual minds; and from their character may that of the whole people be, in certain respects, inferred. Who supposes that the Swiss would have been the same as they are, if Tell's character and deeds could have been hidden in oblivion from the moment

74

those deeds were done? What would the Americans have been now if every impression of Washington could have been effaced from their minds fifty years ago? This is not the place in which to enlarge on the power--the greatest power we know of--which man exercises over men through their affections; but it is a fact which the observer should keep ever in view. The existence of a great man is one of those gigantic circumstances,--one of those national influences,--which have before been mentioned as modifying the conscience-- the feelings about right and wrong--in a whole people. The pursuits of a nation for ever may be determined by the fact of the great man of five centuries being a poet, a warrior, a statesman, or a maritime adventurer. The morals of a nation are influenced to all eternity by the great man's being ambitious or moderate, passionate or philosophical, licentious or self-governed. Certain lofty qualities he must have, or he could not have attained greatness,--energy, perseverance, faith, and consequently earnestness. These are essential to his immortality; upon the others depends the quality of his influence; and upon these must the observer of the present generation reflect.

It is not by dogmas that Christianity has permanently influenced the mind of Christendom. No creeds are answerable for the moral revolution by which physical has been made to succumb to moral force; by which unfortunates are cherished by virtue of their misfortunes; by which the pursuit of speculative truth has become an object worthy of self-sacrifice. It is the character of Jesus of Nazareth which has wrought to these purposes. Notwithstanding all the obscuration and defilement which that character has sustained from superstition and other corruption, it has availed to these purposes, and must prevail more and more now that it is no longer possible to misrepresent his sayings and conceal his deeds, as was done in the dark ages. In all advancing time, as corruption is surmounted, there are more and more who vividly feel that life does not consist in the abundance that a man possesses, but in energy of spirit, and in a power and habit of self-sacrifice: there are perpetually more and more who discern and live by the persuasion that the pursuit of worldly power and ease is a matter totally apart from the function of Christianity; and this persuasion has not been wrought into activity by declarations of doctrine in any form, but by the spectacle, vivid before the eye of the mind, of the Holy One who declined the sword and the crown, lived without property, and devoted himself to die by violence, in an unparalleled simplicity of duty. The being himself is the mover here; and every great man is, in a similar manner, however inferior may be the degree, a spring by which spirits are moved. By the study of them may much of the consequent movement be understood. The observer of British morals should gather up the names of their idols; he will hear of Hampden, Bacon, Shakspeare, Newton, Howard, and Wesley. In Scotland, he will hear of Bruce and Knox. What a flood of light do these names shed on our morale! It is the same with the Englishman abroad when his attention is referred in France to Henri IV, Richelieu, Turenne, and Napoleon, to Bossuet and Fenelon, to Voltaire, and their glorious list of natural philosophers: in Italy, to Lorenzo de' Medici, Galileo, and their constellations of poets and artists: in Germany, to Charles V, Luther, Schwartz, Göthe, Copernicus, Handel, and Mozart. There is in every nation a succession of throned gods, each of whom is the creator of some region of the national mind, and has formed men into more or less of his own likeness.

The other kind of idols are those who are still living, and whose influence upon morals and manners is strong, but may or may not be distinguishably permanent. These afford a less faithful evidence,--but yet an evidence which is not to be neglected. The spirit of the times is seen in the character of the idols of the day, however the nation may be divided in its choice of idols, and however many sects there may be in the man-worship of the generation. In our own day, for instance, how plainly is the movement of society discerned, from the fact of the eminence of philanthropists in many countries! Whether they presently sink, or continue to rise, they testify to a prevailing feeling in society. Père Enfantin in France, Wilberforce in England, Garrison in America,--these are watchmen set on a pinnacle (whoever may object to their being there) who can tell us "what of the night," and how a new morning is breaking. Whether they may be most cause or effect, whether they have more or less decidedly originated the interest of which they are the head, it is clear that there is a certain adaptation between themselves and the general mind, without which they could not have risen to be what they are.--Every society has always its idols. If there are none by merit, at any moment, station is received as a qualification. Large numbers are always worshipping the heads of the aristocracy, of whatever kind they may be; and there is rarely a long interval in which there is not some warrior, some poet, artist, or philanthropist on whom the multitude are flinging crowns and incense. The popularity of Byron testified to the existence of a gloomy discontent in a multitude of minds, as the adoration of De Béranger discloses the political feelings of the French. Statesmen rarely command an overwhelming majority of worshippers, because interest enters much more than sentiment into politics: but every author, or other artist who can reach the general mind,--every preacher, philanthropist, soldier, or discoverer, who has risen into an atmosphere of worship in pursuit of a purpose, is a fresh Peter the Hermit, meeting and stimulating the spirit of his time, and exhibiting its temper to the observer,--foreign as to either clime or century. The physical observer of a new region might as well shut his eyes to the mountains, and omit to note which way the streams run, as the moral observer pass by the idols of a nation with a heedless gaze.

*   *   *   *   *

Side by side with this lies the inquiry into the great Epochs of the society visited. Find out what individuals and nations date from, and you discover what events are most interesting to them. A child reckons from his first journey, or his entrance upon school: a man from his marriage, his beginning practice in his profession, or forming a fresh partnership in trade; if he be a farmer, from the year of a good or bad crop; if he be a merchant, from the season of a currency pressure; if he be an operative, from the winter of the Strike: a matron dates from the birth of her children; her nursemaid from her change of place. Nations, too, date from what interests them most. It is important to learn what this is. The major date of American citizens is the Revolution; their minor dates are elections, and new admissions into the Union. The people at Amsterdam date from the completion of the Stadt Huis; the Spaniards from the achievement of Columbus; the Germans from the deed of Luther; the Haytians from the abduction of Toussaint L'Ouverture; the Cherokees from treaties with the Whites; the people of Pitcairn's Island from the mutiny of the Bounty; the Turks, at present, from the massacre of the Janissaries; the Russians from the founding of St. Petersburgh and the deaths of its monarchs; the Irish (for nearer times than the battle of the Boyne) by the year of the fever, the year of the rebellion, the year of the famine. There is a world of instruction in this kind of fact; and if a new species of epoch, of which there is a promise, should arise,--if the highest works of men should come to be looked upon as the clearest operations of Providence,--if Germany or Europe should date from Göthe as the civilized world does from Columbus,--this sole test might reveal almost the entire moral state of society.

*   *   *   *   *

The treatment of the Guilty is all-important as an index to the moral notions of a society. This class of facts will hereafter yield infallible inferences as to the principles and views of governments and people upon vice, its causes and remedies. At present, such facts must be used with great caution, because the societies of civilized countries are in a state of transition from the old vindictiveness to a purer moral philosophy. The ancient methods, utterly disgraceful as they are, must subsist till society has fully agreed upon and prepared for better ones; and it would be harsh to pronounce upon the humanity of the English from their prisons, or the justice of the French from their galley system. The degrees of reliance upon brute force and upon public opinion are yet by no means proportioned to the civilization of respective societies, as at first sight might be expected, and as must be before punishments and prisons can be taken as indications of morals and manners.

The treatment of the guilty in savage lands, and also in countries under a despotism, indicates the morals of rulers only,--except in so far as it points out the political subservience of the people. It is true that the Burmese must needs be in a deplorable social state, if their king can "spread out" his prime minister in the sun, as formerly described: but the mercy or cruelty of his subjects can be inferred only from the liberty they may have and may use to treat one another in the same manner. In their case, we see that such a power is possessed and put to use. The creditor exposes his debtor's wife, children, and slaves, to the same noon-day sun which broils the prime minister. In Austria, it would be harsh to suppose that subjects have any desire to treat one another as the Emperor and his minister treat political offenders within the walls of the castle of Spielburg. The Russians at large are not to be made answerable for the transportation of coffles of nobles and gentlemen to the silver mines of Siberia, and the regiments on the frontier. It is only under a representative government that prisons, and the treatment of criminals under the law, can be fairly considered a test of the feelings of the majority.

It is too true, however, that punishments are almost everywhere vindictive in their character; and have more relation to some supposed principle of "not letting vice go unpunished," than either to the security of society, or the reformation of the offender. The few exceptions that exist are a far more conclusive testimony to an advancing state of morals than the old methods are to the vindictiveness of the mind of the society which they corrupt and deform. The Philadelphia penitentiary is a proof of the thoughtful and laborious humanity of those who instituted it; but Newgate cannot be regarded as the expressed decision of the English people as to how criminals should be guarded. Such a prison would not now be instituted by any civilized nation. Its existence is to be interpreted, not as a token of the cruelty and profligacy of the mind of society, but of its ignorance of the case, or of its bigoted adherence to ancient methods, or of its apathy in regard to improvements to which there is no peremptory call of self-interest. Any one of these is enough, Heaven knows, for any society to have to answer for; enough to yield, by contrast, surpassing honor to the philanthropy which has pulled down the pillory, and is laboring to supersede the hangman, and to convert every prison in the civilized world into an hospital for the cure of moral disease. But the reform has begun; the spirit of Howard is on its pilgrimage; and barbarous as is still our treatment of the guilty, better days are in prospect.

What the traveller has to observe then is, first, whether there has been any amelioration of the treatment of criminals in countries where the people have a voice upon it: and, in countries despotically ruled, whether public sentiment is moved about the condition of state criminals, and whether men treat one another vindictively in their appeals to the laws of citizenship: whether there is a Burmese cruelty in the exercise of the legal rights of the creditor; whether there is a reluctance to plunge others into the woes of legal penalties; or whether offenders are considered as beyond the pale of sympathy. It may thus appear whether the people entertain the pernicious notion that there is a line drawn for human conduct, on one side of which all is virtue, and on the other all vice; or whether they are approximating to the more philosophical and genial belief that all wickedness is weakness and woe, and that therefore the guilty need more care and tenderness in the arrangement of the circumstances under which they live than those who enjoy greater strength against temptation, and an ease of mind which criminals can never know. In some parts of the United States this general persuasion is remarkably evident, and is an incontestable proof of the advanced state of morals there. In some prisons of the United States, as much care is bestowed on the arrangements by which the guilty are preserved from contaminating one another, are exposed to good influences and precluded from bad, as in any infirmary on the ventilation of the wards, and the diet and nursing of the sick. In such a region, vindictiveness in social punishments must be going out, and Christ-like views of human guilt and infirmity beginning to prevail.

The same conclusions may be drawn from an observation of the methods of legal punishment. Recklessness of human life is one of the surest symptoms of barbarism, whether life is taken by law or by assassination. As men grow civilized, and learn to rate the spiritual higher and higher above the physical life, human life grows sacred. The Turk orders off the head of a slave almost without a serious thought. The New Zealanders have murdered men by scores, to supply their dried and grinning heads to English purchasers, who little imagined the cost at which they were obtained. This is the way in which life is squandered in savage societies. Up to a comparatively high point of civilization, the law makes free with life, long after the private expenditure of it has been checked or has ceased. Duels, brawls, assassinations, have nearly been discontinued, and even war in some measure discountenanced, before the law duly recognizes the sacredness of human life. But the time comes. One generation after another grows up with a still improving sense of the majesty of life,--of the mystery of the existence of such a being as man,--of the infinity of ideas and emotions in the mind of each, and of the boundlessness of his social relations. These recognitions may not be express; but they are sufficiently real to hold back the hand from quenching life. The reluctance to destroy such a creation is found to be on the increase. Men prefer suffering wrong to being accessary to so fearful an act as what now appears a judicial murder: the law is left unused,--is evaded,--and it becomes necessary to alter it. Capital punishments are restricted,--are further restricted,--are abolished. Such is the process. It is now all but completed in the United States: it is advancing rapidly in England. During its progress further light is thrown on the moral notions of a represented people by a change in the character of other (called inferior) punishments. Bodily torments and disfigurements go out. Torture and mutilation are discontinued, and after a while the grosser mental inflictions. The pillory (as mere ignominious exposure) was a great advance upon the maiming with which it was once connected; but it is now discontinued as barbarous. All ignominious exposure will ere long be considered equally barbarous,--including capital punishment, of which such exposure is the recommendatory principle. To refer once more to the Pennsylvania case,--these notions of ignominious exposure are there so far outgrown, that avoidance of it is the main principle of the management. Seclusion, under the guardianship of the law, is there the method,--on the principle of consideration to the weak, and of supreme regard to the feeling of self-respect in the offender,--the feeling in which he is necessarily most deficient. When we consider the brutalizing methods of punishment in use in former times, and now in some foreign countries, in contrast with the latest instituted and most successful, we cannot avoid perceiving that such are indications of the moral notions of those at whose will they exist, be they a council of despots, or an association of nations. We cannot avoid perceiving from them what barbarism is held to be justice in some ages and countries; and how that which would then and there be condemned as culpable leniency, comes elsewhere to be considered less than justice. The treatment of the guilty is one of the strongest evidences as to the general moral notions of society, when it is evidence at all; that is, when the guilty are in the hands of society.

    *   *   *   *   *

There is another species of evidence of which travellers are not in the habit of making use, but which is well worth their attention,--the Conversation of convicted Criminals. There are not many places in the world where it is possible to obtain this, without a greater sacrifice of comfort than the ordinary tourist is disposed to make. There is little temptation to enter prisons where squalid wretches are crowded together in dirt, noise, and utter profligacy; where no one of them could speak seriously for fear of the ridicule of his comrades; where the father sees his young son corrupted before his eyes, and the mother utters cruel jests upon the frightened child that hides its face in her apron. In scenes like these, there is nothing for the stranger to do and to learn. The whole is one great falsehood, where the people are acting falsely under false circumstances. It affords an enterprise for the philanthropist, but no real knowledge for the observer. He may pass by such places, knowing that they are pretty much alike in all countries where they exist. Criminals herded together in virtue of their criminality, and outraged into a diabolical hardihood, must present one uniform aspect of disgust. What variety should there be in them? About as much as in the leper settlements in the wildernesses of the world two thousand years ago.

The traveller will not be permitted to see the state prisoners of any despotic government; but wherever the subject of prison reform has been entertained, (and Howard's spirit is at work in many countries of the world,) there will probably be opportunity to converse with offenders in a better way than by singling them out from the crowd, in a spirit of condescension, and asking them a few questions, in the answers to which you can place no confidence. If you can converse face to face with a convict, as man with man, you can hardly fail to be instructed. If he has been long deprived of equal conversation, his heart will be full; his disposition will be to trust you; his impulse will be to confide to you his offence, and all the details connected with it. By thus conversing with a variety of offenders, you will be put in possession of the causes of crime, of the views of society upon the relative gravity of offences, and of the condition of hope or despair in which those are left who have broken the laws, and are delivered over to shame.

Much light will also be thrown upon the seat of the disorders of society. Putting political offences aside, as varying in number in proportion to the nature of the government, almost all the rest are offences against property. Nine out of ten convicts, perhaps, are punished for taking the money or money's worth of another. Here is a hint as to the respects in which society is most mistaken in its principles, and weakest in its organization. Of the offences against the person, some are occasioned by the bad habits which attend the practice of depredation on property; thieves are drunkards, and drunkards are brawlers:--but the greater number arise out of domestic miseries. Where there are fewest assaults occasioned by conjugal injuries and domestic troubles, the state of morals is the purest. Where they abound, it is clear that the course of love does not run smooth; and that, from the workings of some bad principles, domestic morals are in a low state. In Austria and Prussia, state criminals abound; while in America such a thing is rarely heard of. In America, a youthful and thriving country, offences against property for the most part arise out of bad personal habits, which again are occasioned by domestic misery of some kind; this domestic misery, however, being itself less common than in an older state of society. In England almost all the offences are against property, and are so multitudinous as to warrant a stranger's conclusion that the distribution of property among us must be extremely faulty, the oppression of certain classes by others very severe, and our political morals very low; in short, that the aristocratic spirit rules in England. From the tales of convicts,--how they were reared, what was the nature of the snares into which they fell, what opportunity of retrieving themselves remained, and what was the character of the influences which sank them into misery,--much cannot but be learned of the moral atmosphere

81

in which they were reared. From their present state of mind,--whether they revert in affection to their homes, or to the society from which they have been snatched,--whether they look forward with hope or fear, or are incapable of looking forward at all,--it will appear whether the justice and benevolence of the community have secured the commonest blessings of moral life to these its lowest members, or whether they have been utterly crushed by the selfishness of the society into which they were born. To have criminals at all may in time come to be a disgrace to a community; meantime, their number and quality are an evidence as to its prevalent moral notions, which the intelligent observer will not disregard.

     *   *   *   *   *

[H]"The *songs* of every nation must always be the most familiar and truly popular part of its poetry. They are uniformly the first fruits of the fancy and feeling of rude societies; and, even in the most civilized times, are the only poetry of the great body of the people. Their influence, therefore, upon the character of a country has been universally felt and acknowledged. Among rude tribes, it is evident that their songs must, at first, take their tone from the prevailing character of the people. But, even among them, it is to be observed that, though generally expressive of the fiercest passions, they yet represent them with some tincture of generosity and good feeling, and may be regarded as the first lessons and memorials of savage virtue. An Indian warrior, at the stake of torture, exults, in wild numbers, over the enemies who have fallen by his tomahawk, and rejoices in the anticipated vengeance of his tribe. But it is chiefly by giving expression to the loftiest sentiments of invincible courage and fortitude, that he seeks to support himself in the midst of his torments. 'I am brave and intrepid!' he exclaims,--'I do not fear death nor any kind of torture! He who fears them is a coward--he is less than a woman. Death is nothing to him who has courage!' As it is thus the very best parts of their actual character that are dwelt upon even in the barbarous songs of savages, these songs must contribute essentially to the progress of refinement, by fostering and cherishing every germ of good feeling that is successively developed during the advancement of society. When selfishness begins to give way to generosity,--when mere animal courage is in some degree ennobled by feelings of patriotic self-devotion,--and, above all, when sensual appetite begins to be purified into love,--it is then that the popular songs, by acquiring a higher character themselves, come to produce a still more powerful reaction upon the character of the people. These songs, produced by the most highly-gifted of the tribe,--by those who feel most strongly, and express their feelings most happily,--convey ideas of greater elevation and refinement than are as yet familiar; but not so far removed from the ordinary habits of thinking as to be unintelligible. The hero who devotes himself to death for the safety of his country, with a firmness as yet almost without example in the actual history of the race,--and the lover, who follows his mistress through every danger, and perhaps dies for her sake,--become objects on which everyone delights to dwell, and models which the braver and nobler spirits are thus incited to emulate. The songs of rude nations, accordingly, and those in which they take most pleasure, are filled with the most romantic instances of courage, fidelity, and generosity; and it cannot be supposed that such delightful and elevating pictures of human nature can be constantly before the eyes of any people, without producing a great effect on their character. The same considerations are applicable to the effects of popular ballads upon the most numerous classes of society, even in civilized nations."

It appears that popular songs are both the cause and effect of general morals: that they are first formed, and then react. In both points of view they serve as an index of popular morals. The ballads of a people present us, not only with vivid pictures of the common objects which are before their eyes,-- given with more familiarity than would suit any other style of composition,-- but they present also the most prevalent feelings on subjects of the highest popular interest. If it were not so, they would not have been popular songs. The traveller cannot be wrong in concluding that he sees a faithful reflection of the mind of a people in their ballads. When he possesses the popular songs of former centuries, he holds the means of transporting himself back to the scenes of the ancient world, and finds himself a spectator of its most active proceedings. Wars are waged beneath his eye, and the events of the chase grow to a grandeur which is not dreamed of now. Love, the passion of all times, and the staple of all songs, varies in its expression among every people and in every age, and appears still another and yet the same. The lady of ballads is always worthy of love and song; but there are instructive differences in the treatment she receives. Sometimes she is oppressed by a harsh parent; sometimes wrongfully accused by a wicked servant, or a false knight; sometimes her soft nature is exasperated into revenge; sometimes she is represented as fallen, but always, in that case, as enduring retribution. Upon the whole, the testimony is strong in favor of bravery in men, and purity in women, and constancy in both;--and this in the whole range of popular poetry, from ancient Arabic effusions, through centuries of European song, up to the Indian chants which may yet be heard on the shores of the wide western lakes. The distinguishing attributes of great men bear a strong resemblance, from the days when all Greece rang with the musical celebration of Harmodius and Aristogiton, through the age of Charlemagne, up to the triumphs of Bolivar: and women have been adored for the same qualities, however variously set forth, from the virgin with gazelle eyes of three thousand years ago, to the dames who witnessed the conflicts of the Holy Land, and onwards to the squaw who calls upon her husband not to forget her in the world of spirits, and to our Burns' Highland Mary.

What the traveller has to look to is, that he does not take one aspect of the popular mind for the whole, or a temporary state of the popular mind for a permanent one,--though, from the powerful action of national song, this temporary state is likely to become a permanent one by its means. As an instance of the first, the observer would be mistaken in judging of more than a class of English from some of the best songs they have,--Dibdin's sea songs. They are too fair a representation of the single class to which they pertain, though they have done much to foster and extend the spirit of generosity, simplicity, activity, gaiety, and constant love, which they breathe. They have undoubtedly raised the character of the British navy, and are to a great degree indicative of the naval spirit with us: but they present only one aspect of the national mind. In Spain, again, the songs with which the mountains are ringing, and whose origin is too remote to be traced, are no picture of the conventional mind of the aristocratic classes. As an instance of the false conclusions which might be drawn from the popular songs of a brief period, we may look to the revolutionary poetry of France. It would be unfair to judge of the French people by their ça ira or the Carmagnole, however true an expression such songs may be of the spirit of the hour. The nation had lived before under "une monarchie absolue tempérée par des chansons;" the absolutism grew too galling; and then the songs took the tone of fury which protracted oppression had bred. It was not long before the tone was again changed. Napoleon was harassed on his imperial throne by tokens of a secret understanding, unfriendly to his interests: those tokens were songs ambiguously worded, or set to airs which were used as signs; and treason, which he could not reach, was perpetually spoken and acted within ear-shot and before his eyes. When the royal family returned, the songs of De Béranger passed in like manner from lip to lip, and the restored throne trembled to the echo. In France, morals have for many years found their chief expression in politics; and from the songs of Paris may the traveller learn the political feelings of the time. Under representative governments, where politics are the chief expression of morals, the songs of the people cannot but be an instructive study to the observer; and scarcely less so in countries where, politics being forbidden, the domestic and friendly relations must be the topics through which the most general ideas and feelings will flow out.

The rudest and the most advanced nations abound in songs. They are heard under the plantain throughout Africa, as in the streets of Paris. The boatmen on the Nile, and the children of Cairo on their way to school, cheer the time with chants; as do the Germans in their vineyards, and in the leisure hours of the university. The Negro sings of what he sees and feels,--the storm coming over the woods, the smile of his wife, and the coolness of the drink she gives him. The Frenchman sings the woes of the state prisoner, and the shrewd self-cautionings of the citizen. The songs of the Egyptian are amatory, and of the German varied as the accomplishments of the nation,--but in their moral tone earnest and pure. The more this mode of expression is looked into, the more serviceable it will be found to the traveller's purposes of observation.

      *   *   *   *   *

The subject of the Literature of nations, as a means of becoming familiar with their moral ideas, is too vast to be enlarged on here. The considerations connected with it are so obvious, too, that the traveller to whom they would not occur can be but little qualified for the work of observing.

It is clear that we cannot know the mind of a nation, any more than of an individual, by merely looking at it, without hearing any speech. National literature is national speech. By this are its prevalent ideas and feelings uttered. It is necessarily so; for books which do not meet sympathy from numbers die immediately, and books which strike upon the sympathies of all never die. Between the two extremes, of books which command the sympathies of a class, and those which are the delight of all, there is an extensive gradation, from which the careful observer may almost frame for himself a scale of popular morals and manners. I mean, of course, in countries where there is a copious classical, or a growing modern literature. A people which happens to be without a literature,--the Americans, for instance,--must be judged of, as cautiously as may be, by such other means of utterance as they may have,--the political institutions which the present generation has formed or assented to,--their preferences in selection from the literature of other countries; and so on. But there is a far greater danger of their being misunderstood than there can ever be with regard to a nation which speaks for itself through books. "A country which has no national literature," writes a student of man, "or a literature too insignificant to force its way abroad, must always be to its neighbors, at least in every important spiritual respect, an unknown and misestimated country. Its towns may figure on our maps; its revenues, population, manufactures, political connections, may be recorded in statistical books: but the character of the people has no symbol and no voice; we cannot know them by speech and discourse, but only by mere sight and outward observation of their habits and procedure."[I]

The very fact of there being no literature in a nation may, however, yield inferences as to its mental and moral state. There is a very limited set of reasons why a people is without speech. They are barbarous, or they are politically oppressed; or the nation is young, and busy in providing and securing the means of national existence; or it has the same language with another people, and therefore the full advantage of its literature, as if it were

85

not foreign. These seem to be nearly all the reasons for national silence; and any one of them affords some means of insight into the morals and manners of the dumb people.

As for those which have utterance, they either speak freshly from day to day, or they show their principles and temper by the choice they make from among their own classics. Whatever is most accordant with their sympathies, they dwell upon; so that the selection is a sure indication of what the popular sympathies are. The same may be said of the comparative popularity of modern books; but they may reveal only a temporary state of feeling, and the traveller has to separate this species of evidence from the more important kind which testifies to the permanent affections and convictions of a people. The reveling of the French in Voltaire, of the Germans in Werter, and of the English in Byron, was, in each case, a highly important revelation of popular feeling; but it is not a circumstance from which to judge of the fixed national character of any of the three. It was a sign of the times, and not signs of nations. Voltaire pulled down certain erections which could not stand any longer, and was worshipped as a denier of untruths,--the popular mind being then ripe for the exploding of errors. But here ended the vocation of Voltaire. The French are now busy, to the extent of their energy, in doing what ought to follow upon the exposure of errors;--they are searching after truth. Pretenses having been destroyed, they are now propounding and trying principles; and works which propose new and sounder erections find favor in preference to such as only expose and ridicule old sins and mistakes.--Werter was popular because it expressed the universal restlessness and discontent under which not only Germany, but Europe was suffering. Multitudes found their uncomfortable feelings uttered for them; and Werter was, in fact, the groan of a continent. Old superstitions, tyrannies, and ignorance were becoming intolerable, and no way was seen out of them; and the voice of complaint was hailed with universal sympathy. So it was with the poetry of Byron, adopted and echoed as it was, and will for some time continue to be, by the sufferers under an aristocratic constitution of society, whether they be oppressed by force from without, or by weariness, satiety, and disgust from within. The permanent state of the English mind is not represented in Byron, and could not be guessed at from his writings, except by inference from the woes of a particular order of minds: but his popularity was an admirable sign of the times, for such observers as were capable of interpreting it. Probably, in all ages since the pen and the press began their work, literature has been the expression of the popular mind; but it seems to have become peculiarly forcible, as a general utterance, of late. Whatever truth there may be in speculations about the growing infrequency of "immortal works,"--about the age being past for the production of books which shall become classics,--it appears that literature is assuming more and more the character of letters written to those whom their subjects may concern, and becoming more and more a familiar utterance of the general mind of the day. In the popular modern works of Germany there is deep and warm religious sentiment, while the most unflinching examination into the philosophy and fact of revelation is widely encouraged. In England, there is a growing taste for works which exhibit the life of the lower orders of society, though all aristocratic prepossessions appear in practice as strong as ever. This seems to indicate that our philosophy has a democratic tendency under which a general opinion will be formed, which will, in time, be expressed in practice. The French, again, are devouring, at the rate of two new volumes every three days, novels which are, in fact, letters to those whom they may concern on the condition and prospects of men and women in society. The pictures are something more than mere delineations. They carry with them principles by which the position of the members of the community is to be tested. The social position of Woman is a prominent topic. The first principles of social organization are involved in the groundwork of the simplest stories: and the universal reception of this product of literature shows that those whom it concerns are all. What an enormous loss of knowledge must the traveller sustain who omits to observe and reflect upon the spirit of the fresh literature of a people, or of its preferences among the literature of the past!

He must note whether a people has recent dramatic productions: if not, whether and why the times are unfavorable to that kind of literature; and if there is dramatic production, what are the pictures of life that it presents.

He must obtain at least some general idea of what the mental philosophy of the society is,--not so much because mental philosophy affects the national mind, as because it emanates from it. Is it a gross material, or a refined analytical, or a massy mystical philosophy? The first is usually found in the skeptical stage of the mind of a nation; the last in its healthy infancy; while the other is rarely to be found at all, except as the product of an individual mind of a high order. Few travellers will have occasion to give much attention to this part of their task of observation; as, among all the nations of the earth, there is not one in ten that has any mental philosophy at all.

All have Fiction (other than dramatic); and this must be one of the observer's high points of view. There is no need to spend words upon this proposition. It requires no proof that the popular fictions of a people, representing them in their daily doings and common feelings, must be a mirror of their moral sentiments and convictions, and of their social habits and manners. The saying this is almost like offering an identical proposition. The traveller should stock his carriage with the most popular fictions, whether of the present day, or of a recent or ancient time. He should fill up his leisure with them. He should separate what they have that is congenial with his own habit of mind, from that with which he can least sympathize, and search into the origin of the latter. This will be something of a guide to him as to what is permanent and universal in the sentiments and convictions of the people, and what is to be regarded as a distinctive feature of the particular society or time.

It is impossible but that, by the diligent use of these means, the observer must learn much of the general moral notions of the people he studies,--of what they approve and disapprove,--what they eschew and what they seek,-- what they love and hate, desire and fear;--of what, in short, yields them most internal trouble or peace.

Chapter 3: Domestic State

How lived, how loved, how died they?

Byron

Geologists tell us that they can answer for the modes of life of the people of any extensive district by looking at the geological map of the region. Put a geological map of England before one who understands it, and he will tell you that the inhabitants of the western parts, from Cornwall, through Wales, and up through Cumberland into Scotland, are miners and mountaineers; here living in clusters round the shaft of a mine, and there sprinkled over the hills, and secluded in the valleys. He will tell you that, on the middle portion of the surface, from Devonshire, up through Leicestershire, to the Yorkshire coast, the wide pastures are covered with flocks, while the people are collected into large manufacturing towns; an ordinary map showing, at the same time, that Kidderminster, Birmingham, Coventry, Leicester, and Nottingham, Sheffield, Huddersfield, and Leeds, with many others, lie in this district. He will tell you that the third range, comprehending the eastern part of the island, is studded with farms, and that tillage is the great occupation and interest of the inhabitants.

The moralist might follow up the observations of the geologist with an account of the general characteristics of societies engaged in these occupations. He knows that a distinct intellectual and moral character belongs to miners, to artisans, and to agriculturists; he knows that miners are prone to superstition, and to speculation in business, from the incalculable nature of their pursuits, the hap-hazard character of their enterprises; he knows that an artisan population is active-minded, communicative, capable and fond of concert; that among them is found the greatest proportion of religious dissent and political sagacity, of knowledge and its results in action. He knows that an agricultural people are less of a society than the others; that they are as mentally sluggish in comparison with operatives, as they are physically superior to them; that they make far less use of speech; are more attached to

89

what is habitual and ancient, and have less enterprise and desire of change. They are, in fact, the representatives of the past,--of feudal times; while an artisan population is a prophecy of the future, and the beginning of the fulfillment. The ideas of equal rights, of representation of person as well as property, and all other democratic notions, originate in towns, and chiefly in manufacturing towns. Loyalty to the person rather than the function of rulers, pride in land and love of it as the blessing of blessings, and jealousy of every other interest, are found wherever corn springs up in the furrows, and there are farm-houses to be miniature representations of the old feudal establishments.

Such are the general tendencies, modified according to circumstances. There are influences which make certain artisans in England tories, and certain landlords and tenants liberals; and there may be times and places where whole societies may have their characteristics modified; but there is rarely or never a complete departure from the general rule. Landlords and their posse of tenants, called liberal, soon find a point beyond which they cannot go, and from which they tend back into the politics of their order; and there is often but a single step for tory artisans into ultra-radicalism; it turns out to be a spurious toryism. So it is possible that there might have been here and there a democrat in La Vendée in 1793, and a sprinkling of royalists in Lyons in 1817. Yet La Vendée and Linois may be taken as representatives of the two kinds of society. The weaving population of Lyons are, like that of manufacturing towns generally, disposed to irritability by physical uneasiness, nourishing their ideas and feelings by communication, suffering from the consequences of partial knowledge, having glimpses of a better social state, and laying the blame of their adversities on a deficiency of protection by the government; enterprising and nicely skilled in the improvement of their articles of manufacture, and ever full of aspiration. The inhabitants of La Vendée are so diametrically opposite in their social circumstances and characteristics, that their bias in politics is a matter of course. Here is a description of the face of the district at the time that Lyons was as intensely republican as La Vendée was royalist:--

"Only two great roads traversed this sequestered region, running nearly parallel, at a distance of more than seventy miles from each other. The country, though rather thickly peopled, contained, as may be supposed, few large towns; and the inhabitants, devoted almost entirely to rural occupations, enjoyed a great deal of leisure. The noblesse or gentry of the country were very generally resident on their estates, where they lived in a style of simplicity and homeliness which had long disappeared from every other part of the kingdom. No grand parks, fine gardens, or ornamented villas; but spacious clumsy chateaux, surrounded with farm offices, and cottages for the laborers. Their manners and way of life, too, partook of the same primitive rusticity. There was great cordiality, and even much familiarity, in the intercourse of the seigneurs with their dependents: they were followed by large trains of them in their hunting expeditions, which occupied so great a part of their time. Every man had his fowling-piece, and was a marksman of fame or pretensions. The peasants resorted familiarly to their landlords for advice, both legal and medical; and they repaid the visits in their daily rambles, and entered with interest into all the details of their agricultural operations. From all this there resulted a certain innocence and kindliness of character, joined with great hardihood and gaiety. Though not very well educated, the population were exceedingly devout; though theirs was a kind of superstitious and traditional devotion, it must be owned, rather than an enlightened or rational faith. They had the greatest veneration for crucifixes and images of their saints, and had no idea of any duty more imperious than that of attending on all the solemnities of religion. They were singularly attached also to their curés, who were almost all born and bred in the country, spoke their patois, and shared in all their pastimes and occupations. When a hunting-match was to take place, the clergyman announced it from the pulpit after prayers, and then took his fowling-piece and accompanied his congregation to the thicket."[J]

The chief contrasting features of these two kinds of society may be recognized in all parts of the civilized world. The most intensely loyal of the loyal Chinese will be found irrigating the terraces of the mountains, or busy in the ploughing-matches of the plains; and the least contented will be found at the loom. Spain is removed from a capacity for social freedom just in proportion to the discouragement of manufactures. The vine-growing districts of Germany are the most, and the commercial towns the least, acquiescent in the rule under which they are living. Russia will be despotically governed as long as she has no manufactures; and England and the United States are rescued, by the full establishment of their manufactures, from all danger of a retrogradation towards feudalism.

The way in which these considerations concern us in this place is, that public and private morals, no less than manners, depend on the degree of feudalism which is left in the community. We have spoken before of the morals of the feudal and democratic states of society; and what we are now pointing out is, that these states, with their attendant morals and manners, may be discerned from the face of the country, and the consequent occupations of its inhabitants.

It appears as if a geological map might be a useful guide to the researches of the moralist,--an idea which would have appeared insanely ridiculous half a century ago, but now reasonable enough. If the traveller be no geologist, so that he cannot, by his own observation, determine the nature of the soil, and thence infer, for his general guidance, the employments and mental and moral state of the people, he must observe the face of the country along the road he travels. He will do better still by mounting any eminences which may be within reach, whether they be churches, pillars, pyramids, pagodas, baronial castles on rocks, or peaks of mountains; thence he should look abroad, from point to point, through the whole region, and mark out what he sees spread beneath him. Are there pastures extended to the horizon, with herdsmen and flocks sprinkled over them, and in the midst a cloud of smoke overhanging a town, from which roads part off in many directions? Or is it a scene of shadowy mountains, with streams leaping from their fissures, and no signs of human habitation but the machinery of a mine, with rows of dwellings near heaps of piled rubbish? Or is the whole intersected with fences, and here dark with fallows, there yellow with corn, while farmsteads terminate the lanes, and the dwellings and grounds of rich proprietors are seen at intervals, with each a hamlet resting against its boundaries? Is this the kind of scene, whether the great house be called mansion, or chateau, or villa, or schloss; whether the produce be corn, or grapes, or tea, or cotton? A person gifted with a precocity of science in the twelfth century might have prophesied what is now happening from the picture stretched beneath him as he gazed from an eminence on the banks of the Don or the Calder. He might see, with the bodily eye, only

> Meadows trim with daisies pied,
> Shallow brooks and rivers wide,

with clusters of houses in the far distance, and Robin Hood with his merry men lurking in the thickets of the forest, or basking under the oaks: but with the prophetic eye of science he might discern the multitudes that were, in course of time, to be living in Sheffield or Huddersfield; the stimulus that would be given to enterprise, the thronging of merchants to this region, the physical sufferings, the moral pressure, that must come; the awakening of intelligence, and the arousing of ambition. In the real scene, a cloud-shadow might be passing over a meadow; in the ideal, a smoke-cloud would be resting upon a hundred thousand human beings. In the real scene, a warbling lark might be springing from the grass; in the ideal, a singer[K] of a higher order might appear remonstrating with feudalism from amidst the roar of the furnace-blast and the din of the anvil; and then, when his complaint of social oppression is done, starting forwards to the end of all, and singing the requiem of the world itself.

Whose trade is poaching. Honest Jem works not,
Begs not; but thrives by plundering beggars here.
Wise as a lord, and quite as good a shot,
He, like his betters, lives in hate and fear,
And feeds on partridge because bread is dear.
Sire of six sons apprenticed to the jail,
He prowls in arms, the Tory of the night;
With them he shares his battles and his ale;
With him they feel the majesty of might.
He reads not, writes not, thinks not; scarcely feels:
Steals all he gets; serves Hell with all he steals.

*   *   *   *   *

Yes, and the sail-less worlds which navigate
Th' unutterable deep that hath no shore,
Will lose their starry splendor soon or late,
Like tapers quenched by Him whose will is fate!
Yes, and the angel of Eternity,
Who numbers worlds and writes their names in light,
One day, O Earth, will look in vain for thee,
And start, and stop in his unerring flight;
And with his wings of sorrow and affright
Veil his impassioned brow and heavenly tears!

Somewhat in the same way as such a supposed philosophic observer might be imagined to foresee that democratic strains of remonstrance would here succeed to foresters' and freebooters' songs, may a well-qualified observer of the present day discern the interior mechanism and the remote issues of what lies beneath his eyes. While surveying the vast prairies on the banks of the deep rivers of the Western world, he may safely anticipate the time when self-governing communities will swarm where now a settler's log-house and enclosure are the only break in the wide surface of verdure. While looking down upon the harvests of Volhynia, or watching the processions of wagons laden with corn, and slowly wending their way down to Odessa, he may securely conclude that no vivacious artisan population will enliven this region for a long time to come; that the inhabitants will continue attached to the despotism under which they live; and that the morals of a despotism--the morals which coexist with gross ignorance and social subservience--may be looked for and found for at least an age.

Some preparation may thus be made by a glance over the face of the country. Much depends on whether it is flat or mountainous, pasture or arable land. It appears from fact, too, that much depends on minor circumstances,-- even on whether it is damp or dry. It is amusing to the traveller in Holland to observe how new points of morals spring up out of its swamps, as in the East from the dryness of the deserts. To injure the piles on which the city is built, is at Amsterdam a capital offence; and no inhabitant could outgrow the shame of tampering with the vegetation by which the soil of the dykes is held together. While Irish children are meritoriously employed in gathering rushes to make candles, and sedges for thatch, "the veriest child in Holland would resent as an injury any suspicion that she had rooted up a sedge or a rush, which had been planted to strengthen the embankments."[L] Such are certain points of morals in a country where water is the great enemy. In the East, where drought is the chief foe, it is a crime to defile or stop up a well, and the greatest of social glories is to have made water flow where all before was dry. In Holland, a malignant enemy cuts the dyke, as the last act of malice: in Arabia, he fills up the wells. In Holland, a distinct sort of moral feeling seems to have grown up about intemperance in drink. The humidity of the climate, and the scarcity of clear, wholesome water, obliges the inhabitants to drink much of other liquids. If moderation in them were not made a point of conscience of the first importance, the consequences of their prevalent use would be dreadful. The success of this particular moral effort is great. Drunkenness is almost as rare in Holland as carelessness in keeping accounts, and tampering with the dykes. There is no country in the world whose morals have more clearly grown out of its circumstances than Holland. On the theory of an infallible Moral Sense, it would be as difficult to account for a Dutchman's tenderness of conscience on any of the above three heads, as for a soldier's agony at the imputation of sleeping upon guard, or an Alabama planter's resentment at being charged with putting the alphabet in the way of a mulatto.

     *   *   *   *   *

Having noted the aspect of the country, the observer's next business is to ascertain the condition of the inhabitants as to the supply of the Necessaries of life. He knows that nothing remains to be learned of the domestic morals of people who are plunged in hopeless poverty. There is no foundation for good morals among such. They herd together, desperate or depressed; they have no prospect; their self-respect is prostrated; they have nothing to lose, there is nothing for them to gain by any effort that they can make.--But it is needless to speak of this. When we treat of the domestic morals of any class, it is always presupposed that they are not in circumstances which render total immorality almost inevitable.

In agricultural districts, the condition of the inhabitants may be learned by observation of the markets. An observing traveller has said, "To judge at once of a nation, we have only to throw our eyes on the markets and the fields. If the markets are well supplied, the fields well cultivated, all is right. If otherwise, we may say, and say truly, these people are barbarous and oppressed."[M] This, though a rather sweeping judgment, is founded in truth, and is well worthy of being borne in mind in travelling. It so happens that the negroes of Hayti are abundantly supplied with the necessaries, and with many of the comforts of life; that they are by no means barbarous, and far from being oppressed; and yet they have few roads, and scarcely any markets. They grow up in the midst of plenty; but, when a countryman is about to kill a hog, he sends his son round among his neighbors on horseback, to give notice to any who wish for pork, to send for it on a certain day. Their wretched, barbarous, oppressed countrymen in South Carolina, meanwhile, have excellent markets. The Saturday night's market at Charleston might beguile a careless foreigner into the belief that those who throng it are a free and prosperous people. Thus the rule above quoted does not always hold. Yet it is true that the existence and good quality of markets testify to the existence and good quality of other desirable things.

Where markets are abundantly and variously supplied, it is clear that there must be a large demand for the comforts of life, and a diversity of domestic wants. It is clear that there must be industry to meet this demand, and competence to justify it. There must be social security, or the industry and competence would not be put to so hazardous a use. It may happen, as at Charleston, that the capital is the masters' (whose the profits may also be, at any moment); that the industry is called forth by a delusive hope; and that the briskness of the transactions at market is ascribable to the pleasure slaves have in social meetings; but better things may usually be inferred from a well-supplied and well-conducted market.

*　　*　　*　　*　　*

The traveller's other researches in agricultural regions will be into the Tenure of lands,--whether they are held in small separate properties;--whether such properties are held by individuals, or shared with any kind of partners;--whether portions are rented from landlords; and, if so, whether any order of middlemen are concerned in the business;--whether the land is chiefly held by large owners; and, if so, whether the laborers are attached to the soil under feudal arrangements, or whether they are free laborers working for wages.

The homes of the agricultural population will be found to vary in aspect as any one of these systems prevails. In young and prosperous countries, the system of small separate properties is found to conduce to independence and the virtues which result from it, though it is not favorable to knowledge and enlightenment. Families live much to themselves; and thus, while forming

95

strong domestic attachments, they lose sight of what is going on in the world. They become unused to the light of society, and get to dislike and fear it. The laborers, in such case, usually live with the family, whether they be brothers, as often happens in Switzerland; sons, as in many a farm-house of the United States; or hired servants, as in former times in England,--and still in some retired parts. In each case the picture is easily filled in by the imagination. All are engaged, throughout the year, in the business of living. The work is never ending, still beginning; or, if it has intervals, they are dull and weary, from the absence of interests wherewith to occupy them. The employments of life are innocent, and the principle of association is harmless; but if there be ignorance and prejudice in the region, in these farm-houses will they be found; and in company with them morals of a high order are not to be looked for.

If small properties are held in partnership, poverty is present or threatening. The condition of affairs cannot be lasting; and this may be well; for narrow means and partnership in a property which requires to be managed by skill are more favorable to discontent and disagreement than to a kindly social state.

The middleman system is favorable or unfavorable to morals, just in proportion as it is so to prosperity. Everyone knows the wretchedness of it in Ireland, and that there are numerous instances in Italy of the complete success of the métayer plan.

Where the land is the property of large owners, and is tilled by laborers, there must be more or less of the feudal temper and manners remaining. Where the laborers are attached to the soil, there must necessarily exist whatever good arises from the certainty of the means of subsistence, coupled with the evils of subservience to the will of the lord, mental sluggishness, and ignorance. Where they are not irremovably attached to the soil, habit and helplessness have usually much of the same effect. The son hedges, ditches, or ploughs where his father hedged, ditched, or ploughed; he takes his beer, or cider, or thin wine, (according to the country he lives in,) at the same house of entertainment, and gossips about the doings of the lord and his family, much as laborers were wont to gossip two hundred years ago.

It is the business of the traveller to note which mode of agricultural life prevails, and how the morals which pertain to it are modified by particular circumstances.

    *   *   *   *   *

He must make the same kind of observations on the Manufacturing and Commercial Classes of the country he visits. Here again the chief differences in morals and manners arise out of the comparative prosperity or adversity of the class. Take the cotton manufacture. Passing by the Chinese operative plying his shuttle as he sits under his bamboo shed, and the Hindoo drawing out his fine thread under the shade of the palm, what differences there are among artisans of the same race,--Europeans and of European extraction! In Massachusetts there are villages of artisans, where whole streets of houses are their property; the church on the green in the midst is theirs; the Lyceum, with its library and apparatus, is theirs. There are rows of neat frame-dwellings, painted white or yellow, with piazzas before and behind, and Venetian blinds to every window,--all growing up out of the earnings of girls, who bring their widowed mothers to preside over their establishments. Others are paying off the mortgages on their fathers' farms. Others are procuring for their brothers a learned education in a college. In the cotton settlements of Europe what a contrast! At the best, operatives can only provide for their wants, and the placing out of their children, by a life of strenuous toil. At the worst, they herd together, many families in one house,--often in one room; decency is discarded; recklessness succeeds, to such a degree that, in certain sections of the society, there is scarcely a man of thirty-five who is not a grandfather. Among such there is a barbarism as savage as among the most vicious aristocracy of the worst feudal times. The lowest artisan population of the present day may vie in corruption with the noblesse of France on the eve of the first revolution. It is for the traveller to observe what grade in the wide interval between the operatives of Massachusetts, and those of Lyons and Stockport, is occupied by the artisans of the places he visits.

*   *   *   *   *

Upon the extent of the Commerce of a country depends much of the character of its morals. Old virtues and vices dwindle away, and new ones appear. The old members of a rising commercial society complain of the loss of simplicity of manners, of the introduction of new wants, of the relaxation of morals, of the prevalence of new habits. The young members of the same society rejoice that prudery is going out of fashion, that gossip is likely to be replaced by the higher kind of intercourse which is introduced by strangers, and by an extension of knowledge and interests: they even decide that domestic morals are purer from the general enlargement and occupation of mind which has succeeded to the ennui and selfishness in which licentiousness often originates. A highly remarkable picture of the two conditions of the same place may be obtained by comparing Mrs. Grant's account of the town of Albany, New York, in her young days,[N] with the present state of the city. She tells us of the plays of the children on the green slope which is now State Street; of the tea-drinking and working parties, of the gossip, bickerings, and virulent petty enmities of the young society, with its general regularity and occasional back-sliding; with the gentle despotism of its opulent members, and the more or less restive or servile obedience of the subordinate personages. In place of all this, the stranger now sees a city with magnificent public buildings, and private houses filled with the products of all the countries of the world. The inhabitants are too busy to be given to gossip, too unrestrained in their intercourse with numbers to retain much prudery: social despotism and subservience have become impossible: there is a generous spirit of enterprise, an enlargement of knowledge, an amelioration of opinion. There is, on the other hand, perhaps a decrease of kindly neighborly regard, and certainly a great increase of the low vices which are the plague of commercial cities. Such is the transformation wrought by commerce. An observer who can also speculate,--one who looks before and after,--will conclude that, amidst some evil, the change is advantageous; and that good must, on the whole, arise from enlarged intercourses between men and societies. Seeing in commerce the instrument by which all the inhabitants of the earth are in time to be brought into common possession of all true ideas, and sympathy in all good feelings, he will mark the progress made by the society he visits towards this end. He will mark whether its merchants as a body have a spirit of generous enterprise or of sordid self-interest; whether they entertain a respect for learning and a taste for art,--bringing the one from abroad, and cherishing the other at home;--whether, in short, the merchants are the princes or the money-grubbers of the community. The spirit of this class will determine that of their subordinates. If the masters of commerce are liberal and enlightened, their servants will be thriving, and will have the virtues which wait upon self-respect: if the contrary, they will be debased. A Jewish money-lender is no more like a merchant of Salem or Bourdeaux than Malay porters at Macao are like the clerk class of Amsterdam. In the mercantile orders of society may be found the extremes of honor, generosity, diligence, and accuracy,--and of treachery, meanness, and selfish carelessness. It is the traveller's business to note the tendencies to the one or the other,-- from the vexatious hog and yam traffic of the islands of the South Sea, to the magnificent transactions of the traders of Hamburgh.

*   *   *   *   *

The Health of a community is an almost unfailing index of its morals. No one can wonder at this who considers how physical suffering irritates the temper, depresses energy, deadens hope, induces recklessness, and, in short, poisons life. The domestic affections, too, are apt to languish through disappointment in countries where the average of death is very high. There is least marriage in unhealthy countries, and most in healthy ones,--other circumstances being equal. The same kind of spirit (however largely diluted) prevails in sickly regions as in societies which are visited by a pestilence. Study the tempers of the people who are subject to goîtres, of those who live in marshes, of those who encounter an annual tropical fever; and contrast it with that of dwellers on mountains, and in dry prairies, and in well-ventilated towns. What selfishness, apathy, and discontent in the one class! and what kindliness, briskness, and cheerfulness in the other! In the United States, wide spreading as the country is, and comprehending every variety of people, and almost of climate, the common deficiency of health produces moral effects which must strike the most careless traveller. The epicurean temper of the south, and the puritanic mood of the north, are alike stimulated by this. In the south, the overseers, whose business it is to encounter the fever, seem to be always practically saying, "Let us eat and drink, for to-morrow we die." There is a recklessness among the trading classes there, a heathen levity and grossness, which are doubtless in a great degree owing to the presence of slavery, but also in part to the certainty of a very large annual mortality. Not the purest Christianity itself could preserve a people so placed from a more or less modified fatalism. The richer members of society leave their homes for some months of every year, and go northwards; and this perpetual unsettling of their families has a bad effect upon the habits of the young people and the comfort of their parents. It operates against domestic diligence, tranquility, and satisfaction with home pleasures. In the north, there is a perpetual preaching about death, enforced by the never-ceasing recurrence of it; but it has not the effect of making people less worldly-minded than others. It serves only to shade life with apprehension, uncertainty, and bereavement; and, it is to be feared, to give to the vanity of many minds the direction of false heroism about meeting death. This seems too serious a subject for the exercise of human vanity; yet that purpose it has served, perhaps, in all societies; and in none more than in New England. The greater number of very young people, everywhere, who cannot be aware of the importance of life, and of the simplicity of death as its close, have romantic thoughts about dying early; and, in a country where an unusual proportion do die early, this species of vain-glory is likely to flourish. The pain felt everywhere by really enlarged and religious minds on seeing a false resignation exhibited, and hearing shallow sentimentalities given out on the brink of the grave, is peculiarly felt in a region where mourning mothers may be seen who have lost eight, twelve, or fifteen children, and where scarcely an enterprise of any extent can be undertaken which is not almost sure to be interrupted or baffled by sickness or death.--When these considerations are dwelt upon, and when it is remembered what the consequences of a low state of health must be to each future generation, it seems scarcely extravagant to say that the best influence upon the morals of the American nation would be such as might improve their health.

Good and bad health are both cause and effect of good and bad morals. No proof of this is needed, nor any further dwelling upon the proposition. The fact, however, points out to the observer the duty of obtaining a correct general estimate of the health of the community he visits.

There are two principal methods by which he may obtain the knowledge he wants,--by examining civic registers, and by visiting burial-grounds.

A faithful register of births, marriages, and deaths, is wished for by enlightened philanthropists of all advanced countries, far more as a test of national morals and the national welfare, than as a matter of the highest social convenience. For this the physiologist waits as the means of determining the physical condition of the nation; as a guide to him in suggesting and prescribing the methods by which the national health may be improved, and the average of life prolonged.--For this the legislator waits as the means of determining the comparative proneness of the people to certain kinds of social offences, and the causes of that proneness; that the law may be framed so as to include (as all wise laws should include) the largest preventive influence with the greatest certainty of retribution.--For this the philanthropist waits as a guide to him in forming his scheme of universal education; and without this,-- without knowing how many need education altogether,--how many under one set of circumstances, and how many under another,--he can proceed only in darkness, or amidst the delusions of false lights. He is only perplexed by the partial knowledge, which is all that his utmost efforts enable him to obtain. If he goes into every house of every town and village in his district, he is no nearer to an understanding of the intellectual and moral condition of the nation than he was before: for other districts have a different soil and different occupations; the employments of the people, their diseases and their resources, are unlike; and, under these diverse influences, their physical, and therefore moral and intellectual condition, must vary. The reports of Philanthropic Societies do little more for him, drawn up as they are with partial objects and under exclusive influences: parliamentary disclosures are of little more use. Vague statements about the increase of drunkenness, resistance to one kind of law or another, alarm and distress him; but such statements again are partial, and so often brought forward for a particular object, that they afford no safe guide to him who would form a general preventive or remedy. Thus it is under all partial methods of observation; but when the philanthropist shall gain access to a register of the national births, marriages, and deaths, he will have under his hand all the materials he requires, as completely as if he were hovering over the kingdom, comprehending all its districts in one view, and glancing at will into all its habitations.

The comparative ages of the dead will indicate to him not only the amount of health, but the comparative force of various species of disease; and from the character of its diseases, and the amount of its health, much of the moral state of a people may be safely pronounced upon. The proportion of marriages to births and deaths is always an indication of the degree of comfort enjoyed, and of the consequent purity of morals; and, therefore, of the degree in which education is present or needed. A large number of children, and a large proportion of marriages, indicate physical and moral welfare, and therefore a comparative prevalence of education. A large number of births, and a small proportion of marriages, indicate the reverse. When these circumstances are taken in connection with the prevailing occupations of the district to which they relate, the philanthropist has arrived at a sufficient certainty as to the means of education required, and the method in which they are to be applied.

There is, unfortunately, in all countries, an insufficiency of records framed for the purpose of induction, and subsequent practical use. The chief of a tribe, proud in proportion to his barbarian insignificance, may from time to time indulge himself by numbering the people whom he considers as his property; and an ambitious and warlike emperor may organize a conscription; and these records may remain to fulfill hereafter far more exalted purposes than those for which they were designed: but these instances are few; and in the art of constructing tables, and ascertaining averages, the most civilized people are still, for want of practice, in a state of unskillfulness. But, in the absence of that which would spare observers the task of ascertaining results for themselves, they must take the best they can get. A traveller must inquire for any public registers which may exist in all districts, and note and reflect upon the facts he finds there. In case of there being none such, it is possible that the physicians of the district may be able to afford information from private documents of the same nature. If not, there remain the cemeteries.

The calculators of longevity believe that they may now, by taking down the dates from the first thirty tombstones in the cemeteries of the districts they pass through, learn the comparative healthiness and length of life of the inhabitants of the country. However this may be, there is no doubt that a large variety and extent of information may be thus obtained. The observer can ascertain where the fatal diseases of infancy most prevail,--which is the same thing as knowing that the physical and moral condition of the people is low; as a large proportion (not mere number) of deaths in infancy is a most unfavorable symptom of society. He can ascertain where consumption prevails, where fever, and where the largest proportion attains to length of days. It is much to know what character disease and death wear in any district. One character of Morals and Manners prevails where the greater number die young, and another where they die old; one where they are cut off by hardship; another where they waste away under a lingering disease; and yet another where they abide their full time, and then come to their graves like a shock of corn in its season. The grave-yards on the heights of the Alleghanies

101

will tell a different tale of Morals and Manners from the New Orleans' cemetery, glaring in the midst of the swamp; and so would the burial-places in the suburbs of Irish cities, if their contents were known, from those of the hardy Waldenses, or of the decent and thriving colonists of Frederick's-oord.

    *   *   *   *   *

The Marriage compact is the most important feature of the domestic state on which the observer can fix his attention. If he be a thinker, he will not be surprised at finding much imperfection in the marriage state wherever he goes. By no arrangements yet attempted have purity of morals, constancy of affection, and domestic peace been secured to any extensive degree in society. Almost every variety of method is still in use, in one part of the world or another. The primitive custom of brothers marrying sisters still subsists in some Eastern regions. Polygamy is very common there, as everyone knows. In countries which are too far advanced for this, every restraint of law, all sanction of opinion, has been tried to render the natural method,--the restriction of one husband to one wife,--successful, and therefore universal and permanent. Law and opinion have, however, never availed to anything like complete success. Even in thriving young countries, where no considerations of want, and few of ambition, can interfere with domestic peace,--where the numbers are equal, where love has the promise of a free and even course, and where religious sentiment is directed full upon the sanctity of the marriage state,--it is found to be far from pure. In almost all countries, the corruption of society in this department is so deep and wide-spreading, as to vitiate both moral sentiment and practice in an almost hopeless degree. It neutralizes almost all attempts to ameliorate and elevate the condition of the race.--There must be something fearfully wrong where the general result is so unfortunate as this. As in most other cases of social suffering, the wrong will be found to lie less in the methods ordained and put in practice, than in the prevalent sentiment of society, out of which all methods arise.

It is necessary to make mention (however briefly) of the kinds of false sentiment from which the evil of conjugal unhappiness appears to spring.-- The sentiment by which courage is made the chief ground of honor in men, and chastity in women, coupled with the inferiority in which women have ever been sunk, was sure to induce profligacy. As long as men were brave nothing more was required to make them honorable in the eyes of society: while the inferior condition of women has ever exposed those of them who were not protected by birth and wealth to the profligacy of men.--The shallowness of the sentiment of honor is another great evil. In its origin, honor includes self-respect and the respect of others. In time, "from its intimate connection with what is personal in interest and feeling, it is greatly exposed to degenerate into a false and misguiding sentiment. Connecting itself with the notions of character which prevail by chance in the community, rather than with the rule of right and of God, it has erected a false standard of estimate." The requisitions of honor come to be viewed as regarding only equals, or those who are hedged about with honor, and they are neglected with regard to the helpless. Men of honor use treachery with women,--with those to whom they promise marriage, and with those to whom, in marrying, they promised fidelity, love, and care; and yet their honor is, in the eyes of society, unstained.--Feudal ambition is another sentiment fraught with evil to marriage. In a society where pride and ostentation prevail, where rank and wealth are regarded as prime objects of pursuit, marriage comes to be regarded as a means of obtaining these. Wives are selected for their connections and their fortune, and the love is placed elsewhere.--Any one of these corrupt species of sentiment, and of some others which exist, must ruin domestic peace, if the laws of each country were as wise as they are now, for the most part, faulty, and as powerful as they are now ineffectual.--If the traveller will bear these things in mind, he will gain light upon the moral sentiment of the society by the condition of domestic life in it; and again, what he knows of the prevalent moral sentiment of the society will cast light upon the domestic condition of its members.

Another thing to be carefully remembered is, that asceticism and licentiousness universally coexist. All experience proves this; and every principle of human nature might prophesy the proof. Passions and emotions cannot be extinguished by general rules. Self-mortification can spring only out of a home-felt principle, and not from the will of another, or of any number of others. The exhibition only can be restrained, and the visible conduct ordered by rule. In consequence, it is found that no greater impurity of mind exists than among associated ascetics; and nowhere are crimes of the licentious class so gross, other circumstances being equal, as in communities which have the puritanic spirit. Any one well-informed on the subject is aware that there is much coarseness in the manners of the Quakers; and their regard for the pleasures of the table is open to the observation of all. Nowhere are drunkenness and infanticide more disgusting and horrible, when they do occur, than in Calvinistic Scotland. The bottomless corruption of Vienna is notorious; and much of it is traceable to a species of political asceticism,--to artificial restrictions other than religious, but producing similar effects. Politics are a forbidden topic of conversation. Under this rule, literature is a forbidden topic too; for literary and philosophical necessarily induces political communication. In Vienna may be seen the singular spectacle of an assembled multitude who read, not one of whom opens his lips upon books, or their subject matter. What then remains? Gallantry. The intellect being silenced, the passions run riot; and the excessive corruption of the society,--a corruption which is notorious over the civilized world,--is the natural consequence. It may safely be assumed that wherever artificial restraints are imposed on the passions, or on the intellects and pursuits of men, there must be licentiousness, precisely proportioned to the severity of the restraint.

Celibacy of the clergy, or of any other class of men, involves polygamy, virtual if not avowed, in some other class. To this the relaxation of domestic morals in the higher orders of all Catholic societies bears testimony as strongly as the existence of allowed polygamy in India. It is everywhere professed that Christianity puts an end to polygamy; and so it does, as Christianity is understood in Protestant countries; but a glance at the state of morals in countries where celibacy is the religion of the clergy,--among the higher ranks in Italy, in France, in Spain,--shows that, while the name of polygamy is disclaimed, the thing is held in no great abhorrence. This is mentioned here simply as matter of fact, necessary to our inquiry as to how to observe morals and manners. It is notorious that, wherever celibacy is extensively professed, there is not only, as a consequence, a frequent breach of profession, but a much larger indulgence extended to other classes, in consequence of the restrictions on one. The methods of marriage in Italy and France,--the disposing of the woman at an early age, and before she is capable of giving an enlightened consent,--often even without the form of asking her consent,--on the understanding, tacit or avowed, that she may hereafter place her affections elsewhere,--these proceedings could have been adopted, could now be persevered in, only in countries where partial asceticism had induced a corresponding licentiousness.--The same fact,--the invariable proportion of asceticism and licentiousness,--exists where by some it would be least looked for,--in societies which have the reputation of being eminently pure; and this consideration is sufficient to extinguish all boasting, all assumption of unquestionable moral superiority in one people over another. It is not only that each nation likes its own notions of morals better than those of its neighbors; but that the very same things which are avowed among those who are called the grossest, happen with that which considers itself the most pure. Such superiority as there is is owing, perhaps, in no case to severity of religious sentiment and discipline, but rather to the worldly ease which blesses a young and thinly peopled country, and to the high cultivation of a society which furnishes its members with an extraordinary diversity of interests and pursuits.

Marriage exists everywhere, to be studied by the moral observer. He must watch the character of courtships wherever he goes;--whether the young lady is negotiated for and promised by her guardians, without having seen her intended; like the poor girl who, when she asked her mother to point out her future husband from among a number of gentlemen, was silenced with the rebuke, "What is that to you?"--or whether they are left free to exchange their faith "by flowing stream, through wood, or craggy wild," as in the United States;--or whether there is a medium between these two extremes, as in England. He must observe how fate is defied by lovers in various countries. We have seen what was the acquiescence of Philip and Hannah in their eternal separation. None but Moravians, perhaps, would have so parted forever. Scotch lovers agree to come together after so many years spent in providing the "plenishing." Irish lovers conclude the business, in case of difficulty, by appearing before the priest the next morning. There is recourse to a balcony and rope-ladder in one country; a steam-boat and back-settlement in another; trust and patience in a third; and intermediate flirtations, to pass the time, in a fourth. He must note the degree of worldly ambition which attends marriages, and which may therefore be supposed to stimulate them,--how much space the house with two rooms in humble life, and the country-seat and carriages in higher life, occupy in the mind of bride or bridegroom.--He must observe whether conjugal infidelity excites horror and rage, or whether it is so much a matter of course as that no jealousy interferes to mar the arrangements of mutual convenience.--He must mark whether women are made absolutely the property of their husbands, in mind and in estate; or whether the wife is treated more or less professedly as an equal party in the agreement.--He must observe whether there is an excluded class, victims to their own superstition or to a false social obligation, wandering about to disturb by their jealousy or licentiousness those whose lot is happier.--He must observe whether there are domestic arrangements for home enjoyments, or whether all is planned on the supposition of pleasure lying abroad; whether the reliance is on books, gardens, and play with children, or on the opera, parties, the ale-house, or dances on the green.--He must mark whether the ladies are occupied with their household cares in the morning, and the society of their husbands in the evening, or with embroidery and looking out of balconies; with receiving company all day, or gadding abroad; with the library or the nursery; with lovers or with children.--In each country, called civilized, he will meet with almost all these varieties: but in each there is such a prevailing character in the aspect of domestic life, that intelligent observation will enable him to decide, without much danger of mistake, as to whether marriage is merely an arrangement of convenience, in accordance with low morals, or a sacred institution, commanding the reverence and affection of a virtuous people. No high degree of this sanctity can be looked for till that moderation is attained which, during the prevalence of asceticism and its opposite, is reached only by a few. That it yet exists nowhere as the characteristic of any society,--that all the blessings of domestic life are not yet open to all, so as to preclude the danger of any one encroaching on his neighbor,--is but too evident to the travelled observer. He can only mark the degree of approximation to this state of high morals wherever he goes.

The traveller everywhere finds woman treated as the inferior party in a compact in which both parties have an equal interest. Any agreement thus formed is imperfect, and is liable to disturbance; and the danger is great in proportion to the degradation of the supposed weaker party. The degree of the degradation of woman is as good a test as the moralist can adopt for ascertaining the state of domestic morals in any country.

The Indian squaw carries the household burdens, trudging in the dust, while her husband on horseback paces before her, unencumbered but by his own gay trappings. She carries the wallet with food, the matting for the lodge, the merchandize (if they possess any), and her infant. There is no exemption from labor for the squaw of the most vaunted chief. In other countries the wife may be found drawing the plough, hewing wood and carrying water; the men of the family standing idle to witness her toils. Here the observer may feel pretty sure of his case. From a condition of slavery like this, women are found rising to the highest condition in which they are at present seen, in France, England, and the United States,--where they are less than half-educated, precluded from earning a subsistence, except in a very few ill-paid employments, and prohibited from giving or withholding their assent to laws which they are yet bound by penalties to obey. In France, owing to the great destruction of men in the wars of Napoleon, women are engaged, and successfully engaged, in a variety of occupations which have been elsewhere supposed unsuitable to the sex. Yet there remains so large a number who cannot, by the most strenuous labor in feminine employments, command the necessaries of life, while its luxuries may be earned by infamy, that the morals of the society are naturally bad. Great attention has of late been given to this subject in France: the social condition of women is matter of thought and discussion to a degree which promises some considerable amelioration. Already, women can do more in France than anywhere else; they can attempt more without ridicule or arbitrary hindrance: and the women of France are probably destined to lead the way in the advance which the sex must hereafter make. At present, society is undergoing a transition from a feudal state to one of mutual government; and women, gaining in some ways, suffer in others during the process. They have, happily for themselves, lost much of the peculiar kind of observance which was the most remarkable feature of the chivalrous age; and it has been impossible to prevent their sharing in the benefits of the improvement and diffusion of knowledge. All cultivation of their powers has secured to them the use of new power; so that their condition is far superior to what it was in any former age. But new difficulties about securing a maintenance have arisen. Marriage is less general; and the husbands of the greater number of women are not secure of a maintenance from the lords of the soil, any more than women are from being married. The charge of their own maintenance is thrown upon large numbers of women, without the requisite variety of employments having been opened to them, or the needful education imparted. A natural consequence of this is, that women are educated to consider marriage the one object in life, and therefore to be extremely impatient to secure it. The unfavorable influence of these results upon the happiness of domestic life may be seen at a glance.

This may be considered the sum and substance of female education in England; and the case is scarcely better in France, though the independence and practical efficiency of women there are greater than in any other country. The women in the United States are in a lower condition than either, though there is less striving after marriage, from its greater frequency, and little restriction is imposed upon the book-learning which women may obtain. But the old feudal notions about the sex flourish there, while they are going out in the more advanced countries of Europe; and these notions, in reality, regulate the condition of women. American women generally are treated in no degree as equals, but with a kind of superstitious outward observance, which, as they have done nothing to earn it, is false and hurtful. Coexisting with this, there is an extreme difficulty in a woman's obtaining a maintenance, except by the exercise of some rare powers. In a country where women are brought up to be indulged wives, there is no hope, help, or prospect for such as have not money and are not married.

In America, women can earn a maintenance only by teaching, sewing, employment in factories, keeping boarding-houses, and domestic service. Some governesses are tolerably well paid,--comparing their earnings with those of men. Employment in factories, and domestic service, are well paid. Sewing is so wretched an occupation everywhere, that it is to be hoped that machinery will soon supersede the use of human fingers in a labor so unprofitable. In Boston, Massachusetts, a woman is paid ninepence (sixpence English) for making a shirt.--In England, besides these occupations, others are opening; and, what is of yet greater consequence, the public mind is awakening to the necessity of enlarging the sphere of female industry. Some of the inferior branches of the fine arts have lately offered profitable employment to many women. The commercial adversity to which the country has been exposed from time to time, has been of service to the sex, by throwing hundreds and thousands of them upon their own resources, and thus impelling them to urge claims and show powers which are more respected every day.--In France this is yet more conspicuously the case. There, women are shopkeepers, merchants, professional accountants, editors of newspapers, and employed in many other ways, unexampled elsewhere, but natural and

107

respectable enough on the spot.

Domestic morals are affected in two principal respects by these differences. Where feminine occupations of a profitable nature are few, and therefore overstocked, and therefore yielding a scanty maintenance with difficulty, there is the strongest temptation to prefer luxury with infamy to hardship with unrecognized honor. Hence arises much of the corruption of cities,--less in the United States than in Europe, from the prevalence of marriage,--but awful in extent everywhere. Where vice is made to appear the interest of large classes of women, the observer may be quite sure that domestic morals will be found impure. If he can meet with any society where the objects of life are as various and as freely open to women as to men, there he may be sure of finding the greatest amount of domestic purity and peace; for, if women were not helpless, men would find it far less easy to be vicious.

The other way in which domestic morals are affected by the scope which is allowed to the powers of women, is through the views of marriage which are induced. Marriage is debased by being considered the one worldly object in life,--that on which maintenance, consequence, and power depend. Where the husband marries for connection, fortune, or an heir to his estate, and the wife for an establishment, for consequence, or influence, there is no foundation for high domestic morals and lasting peace; and in a country where marriage is made the single aim of all women, there is no security against the influence of some of these motives even in the simplest and purest cases of attachment. The sordidness is infused from the earliest years; the taint is in the mind before the attachment begins, before the objects meet; and the evil effects upon the marriage state are incalculable.

All this--the sentiment of society with regard to Woman and to Marriage, the social condition of Woman, and the consequent tendency and aim of her education,--the traveller must carefully observe. Each civilized society claims for itself the superiority in its treatment of woman. In one, she is indulged with religious shows, and with masquerades, or Punch, as an occasional variety. In another, she is left in honorable and undisputed possession of the housekeeping department. In a third, she is allowed to meddle, behind the scenes, with the business which is confided to her husband's management. In a fourth, she is satisfied in being the cherished domestic companion, unaware of the injury of being doomed to the narrowness of mind which is the portion of those who are always confined to the domestic circle. In a fifth, she is flattered at being guarded and indulged as a being requiring incessant fostering, and too feeble to take care of herself. In a sixth society, there may be found expanding means of independent occupation, of responsible employment for women; and here, other circumstances being equal, is the best promise of domestic fidelity and enjoyment.

It is a matter of course that women who are furnished with but one object,--marriage,--must be as unfit for anything when their aim is accomplished as if they had never had any object at all. They are no more equal to the task of education than to that of governing the state; and, if any unexpected turn of adversity befalls them, they have no resource but a convent, or some other charitable provision. Where, on the other hand, women are brought up capable of maintaining an independent existence, other objects remain when the grand one is accomplished. Their independence of mind places them beyond the reach of the spoiler; and their cultivated faculty of reason renders them worthy guardians of the rational beings whose weal or woe is lodged in their hands. There is yet, as may be seen by a mere glance over society, only a very imperfect provision made anywhere for doing justice to the next generation by qualifying their mothers; but the observer of morals may profit by marking the degrees in which this imperfection approaches to barbarism. Where he finds that girls are committed to convents for education, and have no alternative in life but marriage, in which their will has no share, and a return to their convent, he may safely conclude that there a plurality of lovers is a matter of course, and domestic enjoyments of the highest kind undesired and unknown. He may conclude that as are the parents, so will be the children; and that, for one more generation at least, there will be little or no improvement. But where he finds a variety of occupations open to women; where he perceives them not only pursuing the lighter mechanic arts, dispensing charity and organizing schools for the poor, but occupied in education, and in the study of science and the practice of the fine arts, he may conclude that here resides the highest domestic enjoyment which has yet been attained, and the strongest hope of a further advance.

* * * * *

Children in all countries are, as Mrs. Grant of Laggan says, first vegetables, and then they are animals, and then they come to be people; but their way of growing out of one stage into another is as different, in different societies, as their states of mind when they are grown up. They all have limbs, senses, and intellects; but their growth of heart and mind depends incalculably upon the spirit of the society amidst which they are reared. The traveller must study them wherever he meets them. In one country, multitudes of them lie about in the streets, basking in the sun, and killing vermin; while the children of the very poorest persons of another country are decently clothed, and either busily occupied with such domestic employments as they are capable of, or at school, or playing among the rocks, or climbing trees, or crawling about the wooden bridges, without fear or danger. From this one symptom, the observer might learn the poverty and idleness of the lower classes of Spain, and the comfort and industry of those of the United States. As to the children of the richer classes, there is the widest difference in the world between those who are the idols of their mothers, (as in societies where the heart's love is lavished on the children which has not been engaged by the husband,) and those who are early steeped in corruption, (as in slave countries,) and those who are reared philosophers and saints, and those to whom home is a sunny paradise hedged round with love and care, and those who are little men and women of the world from the time they can walk alone. All these kinds of children exist,--sure breathings of the moral atmosphere of their homes. The traveller must watch them, talk with them, and learn from their bearing towards their parents, and the bent of their affections, what is the spirit of the families of the land.

From observation on these classes of facts,--the Occupation of the people, the respective Characters of the occupied classes, the Health of the population, the state of Marriage and of Women, and the character of Childhood,--the moralist may learn more of the private life of a community than from the conversation of any number of the individuals who compose it.

Chapter 4: Idea Of Liberty

He who taught man to vanquish whatsoever
Can be between the cradle and the grave,
Crowned him the King of Life. O vain endeavor,
If on his own high will, a willing slave,
He has enthroned the oppression and the oppressor!
What if earth can clothe and feed
Amplest millions at their need,
And power in thought be as the tree within the seed?
Or what if Art, an ardent intercessor,
Diving on fiery wings to Nature's throne,
Checks the great mother stooping to caress her,
And cries, Give me, thy child, dominion
Over all height and depth? If Life can breed
New wants, and wealth from those who toil and groan
Rend of thy gifts and hers a thousandfold for one.

Shelley

The same rule--of observing Things in preference to relying upon the Discourse of persons--holds good in the task of ascertaining the Idea of Liberty entertained and realized by any society. The Things to be observed for this purpose are those which follow.

The most obvious consideration of all is the amount of feudal arrangements which remain,--so obvious as to require only a bare mention. If people are satisfied to obey the will of a lord of the soil, to go out to hunt or to fight at his bidding, to require his consent to marriages among his dependents, and to hold whatever they have at his permission, their case is clear. They are destitute of any idea of liberty, and can be considered at best only half-civilized.--It matters little whether all this subservience is yielded to the owner of an estate, or the sovereign of the country, represented by his police or soldiery. Blind, ignorant obedience to any ruling power which the subjects

111

had no hand in constituting, on the one part, and the enforcement of that obedience on the other, is the feudal temper.

A sleek Austrian of the middle ranks stood, of late, smoking at his door. A practical joker, who had a mind to see how far the man's deference for the police would carry him, drew towards him, and whispered in his ear, "You must dance." The Austrian stared. "Dance, I say!" repeated the stranger, with an air of authority. "Why must I dance?" asked the Austrian, when he had removed the pipe from his mouth. "Because I, an agent of the police, insist upon it." The Austrian instantly began capering, and continued his exercise till desired to stand still, assured that he had satisfied the police.--In the United States, the contrast is amusing. On occasions of public assembly, the appeal is made to the democratic sentiment of the people to preserve order. If an orator is to hold forth on an anniversary, the soldiers (most citizen-like militia) may be seen putting their arms round the necks of newly arrived listeners, in supplication that they will leave seats vacant for the band. If a piece of plate is to be presented to a statesman, and twice as many people throng to the theatre as the building will hold, harangues may be heard from the neighboring balconies,--appeals to the gallantry and kindliness of the crowd,--which are found quite as effectual in controlling the movements of the assemblage as any number of bayonets or constables' staves could be.

This leads to the mention of the Police of a country as a sure sign of the idea of liberty existing within it. Where the soldiery are the guards of social order, it makes all the difference whether they are royal troops,--a destructive machinery organized against the people,--or a National Guard, springing up when needed from among the people, for the people's sake,--or a militia, like the American, mentioned above,--virtually stewards of the meeting, and nothing more. Whatever may be thought of the comparative ease of proceeding, on any given occasion, between a police like that of Paris, and a constabulary like that of the American cities, (a mockery to European rulers,) it is a striking fact that order has been generally preserved for half a century, in a country where public meetings are a hundred times as numerous as in any kingdom in Europe, by means which would in Europe be no means at all. It is clear that the idea of liberty must be elevated, and the love of social order intelligent and strong, where the peace has been kept through unanimity of will. With the exception of outrages growing out of the institution of slavery, (which require a deeper treatment than any species of constabulary can practice,) the United States, with opportunities of disturbance which have been as a hundred to one, have exhibited fewer instances of a breach of public order than any other country in the same space of time; and this order has been preserved by the popular will, in the full knowledge on all hands that no power existed to control this will. This is a fact which speaks volumes in favor of the principles, if not the policy, of the American people.

In the United States, the traveller may proceed a thousand miles in any direction, or live ten years in one place, without the idea of control, beyond that of social convenience, being once presented to his mind. Paul Louis Courier gives us the experience of an acquaintance of his. "Un homme que j'ai vu arrive d'Amérique. Il y est resté trois ans sans entendre parler de ce que nous appelons ici l'autorité. Il a vécu trois ans sans être gouverné, s'ennuyant à périr."--In France, he cannot go in search of the site of the Bastille without finding himself surrounded by watchers before he has stood five minutes.--In Italy, his trunks are opened to examine the books he carries, and compare them with the list of proscribed works.--In Spain, he can say nothing in public that is not likely to be known to the authorities before the day is out; or in private that is not in possession of some priest after the next period of confession.--In Switzerland, he finds that he is free to do anything but make inquiries about the condition of the country. If he asks, as the Emperor Joseph did before him, "Quels sont les revenues de votre république?" he may receive the same answer, "Ils excedent nos dépenses."--In Germany, his case is like that of the inhabitants of the cities;--his course is open and agreeable as long as he pursues inferior objects, but it is made extremely inconvenient to him to gratify his interest in politics.--In Poland, evidences of authority will meet his observation in every direction, while he will rarely hear the name of its head.--In Russia, he will find the people speaking of their despot as their father, and will perceive that it is more offensive to allude to the mortality of emperors than to talk lightly to children of the death of their parents. A gentleman in the suite of an English ambassador inquired, after having been conducted over the imperial palace at St. Petersburgh, which of the rooms he had seen was that in which the Emperor Paul was killed. No answer was returned to his question, nor to his repetition of it. He imprudently persisted till some reply was necessary. His guide whispered, with white lips, "Paul was not killed. Emperors do not die; they transpire out of life."

Such are some of the relations of the people to authority which will strike the observation of the traveller in the most civilized of foreign countries. These will be further illustrated by the smallest circumstances which meet his eye that can in any way indicate what are the functions of the police, and where it has most or least authority. The Emperor Paul issued an ukase about shoestrings, which it was highly penal to disobey. His son has lately ordained the precise measurement of whiskers, and cut of the hair behind, to be observed by the officers of the army. In some regions, all men go armed: in others, it is penal to wear arms: in others, people may do as they please. In some countries, there are costumes of classes enforced by law: in others, by opinion: while fashion is the only dictator in a third. In some societies citizens must obtain leave from the authorities to move from place to place: in others, strangers alone are plagued with passports: in others, there is perfect freedom of locomotion for all.--In his observation of the workings of authority, as embodied in a police, his own experience of restraint or liberty will afford him ample material for thought, and ground of inference.

Such restraint as exists derives its character chiefly from its origin. It makes a wide difference whether the police are the creatures of a despotic sovereign who treats his subjects as property; or whether they are the agents of a representative government, appointed by responsible rulers for the public good; or whether they are the servants of a self-governing people, chosen by those among whom their work lies. It makes a wide difference whether they are in the secret pay of an irresponsible individual, or appointed by command of a parliament, or elected by a concourse of citizens. In any case, their existence and their function testify to the absence or presence of a general idea of liberty among the people; and to its nature, if present.

*   *   *   *   *

It is taken for granted that the traveller is informed, before he sets out, respecting the form of Government and general course of Legislation of the nation he studies. He will watch both, attending upon the administration as well as the formation of laws,--visiting, where it is allowed, the courts of justice as well as the halls of parliament. But he must remember that neither the composition of the government, nor the body of the laws, nor the administration of them, is an evidence of what the idea of liberty at present is among the people, except in a democratic republic, where the acts of the government are the result of the last expression of the national will. Every other representative system is too partial for its legislative acts to be more than the expression of the will of a party; and the great body of laws is everywhere, except in America, the work of preceding ages. Though, therefore, the observer will allow no great legislative and administrative acts to pass without his notice, he will apply himself to other sets of circumstances to ascertain what is the existing idea of liberty prevalent among the people. He will observe, from certain facts of their position, what this idea must be; and, from certain classes of their own deeds, what it actually is.

 One of the most important circumstances is, whether the population is thinly sprinkled over the face of the country, or whether it is collected into neighborly societies. This all-important condition has been alluded to so often already that it is only necessary to remind the observer never to lose sight of it. "Plus un peuple nombreux se rapproche," says Rousseau, "moins le gouvernement peut usurper sur le souverain. L'avantage d'un gouvernement tyrannique est donc en ceci, d'agir à grandes distances. A l'aide des points d'appui qu'il se donne, sa force augmente au loin, comme celle des léviers.

Celle du peuple, au contraire, n'agit que concentrée: elle s'évapore et se perd en s'étendant, comme l'effet de la poudre éparse à terre, et qui ne prend feu que grain à grain. Les pays les moins peuplés sont ainsi les plus propres à la tyrannie. Les bêtes féroces ne règnent que dans les déserts."

It is obvious enough that the Idea of Liberty, which can originate only in the intercourse of many minds, as the liberty itself can be wrought out only by the labors of many united hands, is not to be looked for where the people live apart, and are destitute of any knowledge of the interests and desires of the community at large.

      *   *   *   *   *

Whether the society is divided into Two Classes, or whether there is a Gradation, is another important consideration. Where there are only two, proprietors and laborers, the Idea of Liberty is deficient or absent. The proprietary class can have no other desires on the subject than to repress the encroachments of the sovereign above them, or of the servile class below them: and in the servile class the conception of liberty is yet unformed. Only in barbarous countries, in countries where slavery subsists, and in some few strongholds of feudalism, is this decided division of society into two classes now to be found. Everywhere else there is more or less gradation; and in the most advanced countries the classes are least distinguishable. Below those members who, in European societies, are distinguished by birth, there is class beneath class of capitalists, though it is usual to comprehend them all, for convenience of speech, under the name of the middle class. Thus society in Great Britain, France, and Germany is commonly spoken of as consisting of three classes; while the divisions of the middle class are, in fact, very numerous. The small shopkeeper is not of the same class with the landowner, or wealthy banker, or professional man; while their views of life, their political principles, and their social aspirations, are as different as those of the peer and the mechanic.

There are two pledges of the advancement of the idea of liberty in a community:--the one is the mingling of the functions of proprietor and laborer throughout the whole of a society ruled by a representative government; the other is the graduation of ranks by some other principle than hereditary succession.

In ancient times most men were proprietors and laborers too; but under despotic rule. Societies which have once come under the representative principle are not likely to retrograde to this state; while there are influences ever at work to exalt the function of labor, and to extend that of proprietorship. Wherever this mixture of functions has gone the furthest,-- wherever the mechanic classes are becoming capitalists, and proprietors are liable to sink down from their ancient honor, unless they can secure respect by personal qualifications, the idea of liberty is, to a considerable degree, confirmed and elevated. In such a case, it is clear that both the power and the desire of encroachment on the part of the upper class must be lessened, and that of resistance on the part of the lower increased.--The other improvement follows upon this. Proprietorship, with its feudal influences, having lost caste (though it has gained in true dignity), some other ground of distinction must succeed. If we may judge by what is before our eyes in the Western world, talent is likely to be the next successor. It is to be hoped that talent will, in its turn, give way to moral worth,--the higher degrees of which imply, however, superiority of mental power. The preference of personal qualifications to those of external endowment has already begun in the world, and is fast making its way. Such distinction of ranks as there is in America originates in mental qualifications. Statesmen, who rise by their own power, rank highest; and then authors. The wealthiest capitalist gives place, in the estimation of all, to a popular orator, a successful author, or an eminent clergyman.--In France, the honors of the peerage and the offices of the state are given to men of science, philosophy, and literature. The same is the case in some parts of Germany: and, even in aristocratic England, the younger members of her Upper House are unsatisfied with being merely peers, and are anxious to push their way in literature, as well as in politics.--The traveller must give earnest heed to symptoms like these, knowing that as the barriers of ranks are thrown down, and personal obtain the ascendant over hereditary qualifications, social coercion must be relaxed, and the sentiment of liberty exalted.

    *   *   *   *   *

In close connection with this, he must observe the condition of Servants. The treatment and conduct of domestics depend on causes which lie far deeper than the principles and tempers of particular servants and masters, as may be seen by a glance at domestic service in England, Scotland, and Ireland. In England, the old Saxon and Norman feud smoulders, (however unconscious the parties may be of the fact,) in the relation of master and servant. Domestics who never heard of either Norman or Saxon entertain a deep-rooted conviction of their masters' interests and their own being directly opposed, and are subject to a strong sense of injury. Masters who never bestow a thought on the transactions of the twelfth century, complain of a doggedness, selfishness, and case-hardened indifference in the class of domestics, which kindness cannot penetrate, or penetrates only to pervert. The relation is therefore a painful one in England. There is little satisfaction to be obtained between the extremes of servility and defiance, by which the conduct of servants is almost as distinctly marked now as when the nation was younger by seven centuries. The English housewives complain that confidence only makes their maid servants conceited, and that indulgence spoils them.--In Ireland, the case is of the same nature, but much aggravated. The injury of having an aristocracy of foreigners forced on the country, to whom the natives are to render service, is more recent, and the impression more consciously retained. The servants are ill-treated, and they yield bad service in return. It is mournful to see the arrangement of Dublin houses. The drawing-rooms are palace-like, while the servants' apartments are dark and damp dungeons. It is wearisome to hear the complaints of the dirt, falsehood, and faithlessness of Irish servants,--complaints which their mistresses have ever ready for the ear of the stranger; and it is disgusting to witness the effects in the household. It is equally sad and ludicrous to see the mistress of some families enter the breakfast room, with a loaf of bread under her arm, the butter-plate in one hand, and a bunch of keys in the other;--to see her cut from the loaf the number of slices required, and send them down to be toasted,-- explaining that she is obliged to lock up the very bread from the thievery of her servants, and informing against them as if she expected them to be worthy of trust, while she daily insults them with the refusal of all trust,--even to the care of the bread-pan. In Scotland, the case is widely different. Servitude and clanship are there connected, instead of servitude and conquest. The service is willing in proportion; and the faults of domestics are not those common to the oppressed, but rather those proceeding from pride and self-will. The Scotch domestic has still the pride in the chief of the name which cherishes the self-respect of every member of a clan; and in the service of the chief there is scarcely any exertion which the humblest of his name would not make. The results are obvious. There is a better understanding between the two classes than in the other divisions of the kingdom: and Scotch masters and mistresses obtain a satisfaction from their domestics which no degree of justice and kindness in English and Irish housekeepers can secure. The dregs of an oppression of centuries cannot be purged away by the action of individual tempers, be they of the best. The causes of misunderstanding, as we have said, lie deep.

The principles which regulate the condition of domestic servants in every country form thus a deep and wide subject for the traveller's inquiries. In America, he will hear frequent complaints from the ladies of the pride of their maid servants, and of the difficulty of settling them, while he sees that some are the most intimate friends of the families they serve; and that not a few collect books, and attend courses of scientific lectures. The fact is that, in America, a conflict is going on between opposite principles, and the consequences of the struggle show themselves chiefly in the relation between master and servant. The old European notions of the degradation of servitude survive in the minds of their American descendants, and are nourished by the presence of slavery on the same continent, and by the importation of laborers from Europe which is perpetually going on. In conflict with these notions are the democratic ideas of the honorableness of voluntary service by contract. It is found difficult, at first, to settle the bounds of the contract; and masters are liable to sin, from long habit, on the side of imperiousness, and the servants on that of captiousness and jealousy of their own rights. Such are the inconveniences of a transition state;--a state, however, upon which it should be remembered that other societies have yet to enter. In an Irish country-house, the guest sometimes finds himself desired to keep his wardrobe locked up.--In England, he perceives a restraint in the address of each class to the class above it.--In France, a washerwoman speaks with as much ease to a duchess as a duchess to a washerwoman.--In Holland, the domestics have chambers as scrupulously neat as their masters'.--In Ireland, they sleep in underground closets.--In New York, they can command their own accommodation.--In Cuba they sleep, like dogs, in the passages of the family dwellings. These are some of the facts from which the observer is to draw his inferences, rather than from the manners of some individuals of the class whom he may meet. In his conclusions from such facts he can hardly be wrong, though he may chance to become acquainted with a footman of the true heroic order in Dublin, and a master in Cuba who respects his own servants, and a cringing lackey in New York.

*   *   *   *   *

A point of some importance is whether the provincial inhabitants depend upon the management and imitate the modes of life of the metropolis, or have principles and manners of their own. Where there is least freedom and the least desire of it, everything centers in the metropolis. Where there is most freedom, each "city, town, and vill," thinks and acts for itself. In despotic countries, the principle of centralization actuates everything. Orders are issued from the central authorities, and the minds of the provinces are saved all trouble of thinking for themselves. Where self-government is permitted to each assemblage of citizens, they are stimulated to improve their idea and practice of liberty, and are almost independent of metropolitan usages. The traveller will find that "Paris is France," as everybody has heard, and that the government of France is carried on in half-a-dozen apartments in the capital, with little reference to the unrepresented thousands who are living some hundreds of miles off: while, if he casts a glance over Norway, he may see the people on the shores of the fiords, or in the valleys between the pine-steeps, quietly making their arrangements for controlling the central authority, even abolishing the institution of hereditary nobility in opposition to the will of the king; but legally, peaceably, and in all the simplicity of determined independence,--the result of a matured idea of liberty. The observer will note whether the pursuits and amusements of the provincial inhabitants originate in the circumstances of the locality, or whether they are copies from those of the metropolis; whether the great city be spoken of with reverence, scorn, or indifference, or not spoken of at all: whether, as in a Pennsylvanian village, the society could go on if the capital were swallowed up by an earthquake; or whether, as in Prussia, the favor of the central power is as the breath of the nostrils of the people.

*　　*　　*　　*　　*

Newspapers are a strong evidence of the political ideas of a people;--not individual newspapers; for no two, perhaps, fully agree in principles and sentiment, and it is to be feared that none are positively honest. Not by individual newspapers must the traveller form his judgment, but by the freedom of discussion which he may find to be permitted, or the restraints upon discussion imposed. The idea of liberty must be low and feeble among a people who permit the government to maintain a severe censorship; and it must be powerful and effectual in a society which can make all its complaints through a newspaper,--be the reports of the newspapers upon the state of social affairs as dismal as they may. Whatever revilings of a tyrannical president, or of a servile congress, a traveller may meet with in any number of American journals, he may fairly conclude that both the one and the other must be nearly harmless if they are discussed in a newspaper. The very existence of the newspapers he sees testifies to the prevalence of a habit of reading, and consequently of education--to the wide diffusion of political power--and to the probable safety and permanence of a government which is founded on so broad a basis, and can afford to indulge so large a license. Whatever he may be told of the patriotism of a sovereign, let him give it to the winds if he finds a space in a newspaper made blank by the pen of a censor. The tameness of the Austrian journals tells as plain a tale as if no censor had ever suppressed a syllable;--as much so as the small size of a New Orleans paper compared with one of New York, or as the fiercest bluster of a Cincinnati Daily or Weekly, on the eve of the election of a president.

*　　*　　*　　*　　*

In countries where there is any Free Education, the traveller must observe its nature; and especially whether the subjects of it are distinguished by any sort of badge. The practice of badging, otherwise than by mutual consent, is usually bad: it is always suspicious. The traveller will note whether free education is conferred by charitable bequest, (a practice originating in times when the doctrine of expiation was prevalent, and continued to this day by its union with charity,) or whether it is framed at the will of the sovereign, that his young subjects may be trained to his own purposes,--as in the case of the Emperor of Russia and his young Polish victims; or whether it arises from the union of such a desire with a more enlightened object,--as may be witnessed

119

in Prussia; or whether it is provided by the sovereign people,--by universal consent, as the right of every individual born into the community, and as the necessary qualification for the enjoyment of social privileges,--as in the United States. The English Christ Hospital boys are badged: Napoleon's Polytechnic pupils were badged; so are the Czar's orphan charge. Wherever the meddling or ostentatious charity of antique times is in existence,--times when the idea of liberty was low and confined,--this badging is to be looked for; and also wherever it is necessary to the purposes of the potentate to keep a register of the young subjects who may become his instruments or his foes:--but where education is absolutely universal, where any citizen has a right to put every child, not otherwise educated, into the school-house of his township, and where the rising generation are destined to take care of themselves, and legislate after their own will, no badging will be found. This apparently trifling fact is worth the attention of the observer.

The extent of popular education is a fact of the deepest significance. Under despotisms there will be the smallest amount of it; and in proportion to the national idea of the dignity and importance of man,--idea of liberty, in short,--will be its extent, both in regard to the number it comprehends, and to the enlargement of their studies. The universality of education is inseparably connected with a lofty idea of liberty; and till the idea is realized in a constantly expanding system of national education, the observer may profitably note for reflection the facts whether he is surrounded on a frontier by a crowd of whining young beggars, or whether he sees a parade of charity scholars,--these all in blue caps and yellow stockings, and those all in white tippets and green aprons; or whether he falls in with an annual or quarterly assembly of teachers, met to confer on the best principles and methods of carrying on an education which is itself a matter of course.

In countries where there is any popular Idea of Liberty, the universities are considered its stronghold, from their being the places where the young, active, hopeful, and aspiring meet,--the youths who are soon to be citizens, and who have here the means of daily communication of their ideas, for many years together. It would be an interesting inquiry how many revolutions, warlike or bloodless, have issued from seats of learning; and yet more, how many have been planned for which the existing powers, or the habits of society, have been too strong. If the universities are not so constituted as to admit of this fostering of free principles, they are pretty sure to retain the antique notions in accordance with which they were instituted, and to fall into the rear of society in morals and manners. It is the traveller's business to observe the characteristics of these institutions, and to reflect whether they are likely to aid or to retard the progress of the nation in which they stand.

There are universities in almost every country; but they are as little like one another as the costumes that are found in Switzerland and India; and the one speak as plainly of morals and manners as the other of climate. It is needless to point out that countries which contain only aristocratic halls of learning, or schools otherwise devoid of an elastic principle, must be in a state of comparative barbarism; because, in such a case, learning (so called there) must be confined to a few, and probably to the few who can make the least practical use of it. Where the universities are on such a plan as that, preserving their primary form, they can admit increasing numbers, the state of intellect is likely to be a more advanced one. But a more favorable symptom is where seats of learning are multiplied as society enlarges, modified in their principles as new departments of knowledge open, and as new classes arise who wish to learn. That country is in a state of transition--of progression-- where the ancient universities are honored for as much as they can give, while new schools arise to supply their deficiencies, and Mechanics' Institutes, or some kindred establishments, flourish by the side of both. This state of things, this variety in the pursuit of knowledge, can exist only where there is a freedom of thought, and consequent diversity of opinion, which argues a vigorous idea of liberty.

The observer must not, however, rest satisfied with ascertaining the proportion of the means of education to the people who have to be educated. He must mark the objects for which learning is pursued. The two most strongly contrasted cases which can be found are probably those of Germany and (once more) the United States. In the United States, it is well known, a provision of university education is made as ample as that of schools for an earlier stage; yet no one pretends that a highly finished education is to be looked for in that country. The cause is obvious. In a young nation, the great common objects of life are entered upon earlier, and every preparatory process is gone through in a more superficial manner. Seats of learning are numerous and fully attended, both in Germany and America, and they testify in each to a pervading desire of knowledge. Here the agreement ends. The German student may, without being singular, remain within the walls of his college till time silvers his hairs; or he has even been known to pass eighteen years among his books, without once crossing the threshold of his study. The young American, meanwhile, satisfied at the end of three years that he knows as much as his neighbors, settles in a home, engages in farming or commerce, and plunges into what alone he considers the business of life. Each of these pursues his appropriate objects: each is right in his own way: but the difference of pursuit indicates a wider difference of sentiment between the two countries than the abundance of the means of learning in each indicates a resemblance. The observer must therefore mark, not only what and how many are the seats of learning, but who frequent them; whether there are many, past

121

the season of youth, who make study the business of their lives; or whether all are of that class who regard study merely as a part of the preparation which they are ordained to make for the accomplishment of the commonest aims of life. He can scarcely take his evening walk in the precincts of a university without observing a difference so wide as this.

The great importance of the fact lies in this,--that increase of knowledge is necessary to the secure enlargement of freedom. Germany may not, it is true, require learning in her youth for political purposes, but because learning has become the taste, the characteristic honor of the nation; but this knowledge will infallibly work out, sooner or later, her political regeneration. America requires knowledge in her sons because her political existence itself depends upon their mental competency. The two countries will probably approximate gradually towards a sympathy which is at present out of the question. As America becomes more fully peopled, a literature will grow up within her, and study will assume its place among the chief objects of life. The great ideas which are the employment of the best minds of Germany must work their way out into action; and new and immediately practical kinds of knowledge will mingle themselves, more and more largely, with those to which she has been, in times past, devoted. The two countries may thus fall into a sympathetic correspondence on the mighty subjects of human government and human learning, and the grand idea of liberty may be made more manifest in the one, and disciplined and enriched in the other.

       *   *   *   *   *

One great subject of observation and speculation remains--the objects and form of Persecution for Opinion in each country. Persecution for opinion is always going on among a people enlightened enough to entertain any opinions at all. There must always be, in such a nation, some who have gone further in research than others, and who, in making such an advance, have overstepped the boundaries of popular sympathy. The existence and sufferings of such are not to be denied because there are no fires at the stake, and no organized and authorized Inquisition, and because formal excommunication is gone out of fashion. Persecution puts on other forms as ages elapse; but it is not extinct. It can be inflicted out of the province of law, as well as through it; by a neighborhood as well as from the Vatican. A wise and honest man may be wounded through his social affections, and in his domestic relations, as effectually as by flames, fetters, and public ignominy. There are wise and good persons in every civilized country, who are undergoing persecution in one form or another every day.

Is it for precocity in science? or for certain opinions in politics? or for a peculiar mode of belief in the Christian religion, or unbelief of it? or for championship of an oppressed class? or for new views in morals? or, for fresh inventions in the arts, apparently interfering with old-established interests? or for bold philosophical speculation? Who suffers arbitrary infliction, in short, and how, for any mode of thinking, and of faithful action upon thought? An observer would reject whatever he might be told of the paternal government of a prince, if he saw upon a height a fortress in which men were suffering carcere duro for political opinions. In like manner, whatever a nation may tell him of its love of liberty should go for little if he sees a virtuous man's children taken from him on the ground of his holding an unusual religious belief; or citizens mobbed for asserting the rights of negroes; or moralists treated with public scorn for carrying out allowed principles to their ultimate issues; or scholars oppressed for throwing new light into the sacred text; or philosophers denounced for bringing fresh facts to the surface of human knowledge, whether they seem to agree or not with long-established suppositions.

The kind and degree of infliction for opinion which is possible, and is practiced in the time and place, will indicate to the observer the degree of imperfection in the popular idea of liberty. This is a kind of fact easy to ascertain, and worthy of all attention.

Chapter 5: Progress

'Tis the sublime of man,
Our noontide majesty, to know ourselves
Parts and proportions of one wondrous whole!
This fraternizes man, this constitutes
Our charities and bearings.

Coleridge

Then let us pray that come it may,
As come it will for a' that,
That sense and worth, o'er a' the earth,
May bear the gree, and a' that.
For a' that, and a' that,
It's coming yet, for a' that,
That man to man, the warld o'er,
Shall brothers be for a' that.

Burns

However widely men may differ as to the way to social perfection, all whose minds have turned in that direction agree as to the end. All agree that if the whole race could live as brethren, society would be in the most advanced state that can be conceived of. It is also agreed that the spirit of fraternity is to be attained, if at all, by men discerning their mutual relation, as "parts and proportions of one wondrous whole." The disputes which arise are about how these proportions are to be arranged, and what those qualifications should be by which some shall have an ascendancy over others.

This cluster of questions is not yet settled with regard to the inhabitants of any one country. The most advanced nations are now in a condition of internal conflict upon them. As for the larger idea,--that nations as well as individuals are "parts and proportions of one wondrous whole," it has hardly yet passed the lips or pen of any but religious men and poets. Its time will come when men have made greater progress, and are more at ease about the domestic arrangements of nations. As long as there are, in every country of the world, multitudes who cannot by any exertion of their own redeem themselves from hardship, and their children from ignorance, there is quite enough for justice and charity to do at home. While this is doing,--while the English are striving to raise the indigent classes of their society, the French speculating to elevate the condition of woman, and to open the career of life to all rational beings, the Germans waiting to throw off the despotism of absolute rulers, and the Americans struggling to free the negroes,--the fraternal sentiment will be growing, in preparation for yet higher results. The principle, acted upon at home, will be gaining strength for exercise abroad; and the more any society becomes like a band of brothers, the more powerful must be the sympathy which it will have to offer to other such bands.

Far off as may be the realization of such a prospect, it is a prospect. For many ages poets and philosophers have entertained the idea of a general spirit of fraternity among men. It is the one great principle of the greatest religion which has ever nourished the morals of mankind. It is the loftiest hope on which the wisest speculators have lived. Poets are the prophets, and philosophers the analyzers of the fate of men, and religion is the promise and pledge of unseen powers to those who believe in them. That cannot be unworthy of attention, of hope, of expectation, which the poets and the analyzers of the race, have reposed upon, and on which the best religion of the world (and that which comprehends all others) is based. That which has never, for all its splendor, been deemed absurd by the wisest of the race is now beginning to be realized. We have now something more to show for our hope than what was before enough for the highest minds. The fraternal spirit has begun to manifest itself by its workings in society. The helpless are now aided expressly on the ground of their helplessness,--not from the emotions of compassion excited by the spectacle of suffering in particular cases, but in a nobler and more abstract way. Classes, crowds, nations of sufferers are aided and protected by strangers, powerful and at ease, who never saw an individual of the suffering thousands, and who have none but a spiritual interest in their welfare. Since missions to barbarous countries, action against slavery, and the care of the blind, deaf and dumb, and paupers, have become labors of society, the fraternity of men has ceased to be a mere aspiration, or even prophecy and promise. It is not only that the high-placed watchmen of the world have announced that the day is coming,--it has dawned; and there is every reason to expect that it will brighten into noon.

The traveller must be strangely careless who, in observing upon the morals of a people, omits to mark the manifestations of this principle;--to learn what is its present strength, and what the promise of its growth. By fixing his observation on this he may learn, and no otherwise can he learn, whether the country he studies is advancing in wisdom and happiness, or whether it is stationary, or whether it is going back. The probabilities of its progress are wholly dependent upon this.--It will not take long to point out what are the signs of progression which he must study.

*   *   *   *   *

It is of great consequence whether the nation is insular or continental, independent or colonial. Though the time seems to be come when the sea is to be made a highway, as easy of passage as the land, such has not been the case till now. Even in the case of Great Britain,--the most accessible of islands, and the most tempting to access,--before the last series of wars, a much smaller number of strangers visited her than could have been supposed to come if they had only to pass land frontiers. During the wars, she was almost excluded from continental society. The progress that her people have made in liberality and humanity since communication has been rendered easy, is so striking that it is impossible to avoid supposing the enlarged commerce of mind which has taken place to be one of the chief causes of the improvement. It is probable that the advancement of the nation would have been still greater if the old geological state of junction with the continent had been restored for the last twenty years. She would then have been almost such a center of influx as France has been, and by which France has so far profited that the French are now, it is believed, the most active-minded and morally progressive nation in the world. Much of the vigor and progression of France is doubtless owing to other causes; but much also to her rapid and extensive intercourse with the minds of many nations. The condition of the inhabitants of other islands is likely to be less favorable to progression than that of the British, in proportion as they have less intercourse. They are likely to have even more than the English proportion of self-satisfaction, dislike of foreigners, and reserve. Generally speaking, the inhabitants of islands are found to be to those of continental countries as villagers to citizens: they have good qualities of their own, but are behind the world. Malta has not the chance that she would have if we could annex her to the South of France; nor will the West India islands advance as they would do if we could throw them all into one, and intersect the whole with roads leading on either side from the great European and American cities.

Malta and the West India islands have, however, the additional disadvantage of being colonies. The moral progression of a people can scarcely begin till they are independent. Their morals are overruled by the mother-country,--by the government and legislation she imposes, by the rulers she sends out, by the nature of the advantages she grants and the tribute she requires, by the population she pours in from home, and by her own example. Accordingly, the colonies of a powerful country exhibit an exaggeration of the national faults, with only infant virtues of their own, which wait for freedom to grow to maturity, and among which an enlarged sympathy with the race is seldom found. This is a temper uncongenial with a confined, dependent, and imitative society; and the first strong symptoms of it are usually found in the persons of those whose mission it is to lead the colony out of its minority into independence.

These are conditions of a people which may guide the traveller's observations by showing him what to expect. Remembering these conditions, he will mark the greater or less enlargement and generosity of the spirit of society, and learn from these the fact or promise of progression, or whether it is too soon to look for either.

There is another important condition which can hardly escape his notice: whether the people are homogeneous or composed of various races. The inhabitants of New England are a remarkable specimen of the first, as the inhabitants of the middle states of America will be of the last, two or three generations hence. Almost all the nations of Europe are mongrel; and those which can trace their descent from the greatest variety of ancestors have, other circumstances remaining the same, the best chance of progression. Among a homogeneous people, ancestral virtues flourish; but these carry with them ancestral faults as their shadow; and there is a liability of a new fault being added,--resistance to the spirit of improvement. If the chances of severity of ancient virtue are lessened in the case of a mongrel people, there is a counterbalancing advantage in the greater diversity of interests, enlargement of sympathy, and vigor of enterprise introduced by the close union of the descendants of different races. The people of New England, almost to a man descended from the pilgrim fathers, have the strong religious principle and feeling, the uprightness, the domestic attachment, and the principled worldly prudence of their ancestors, with much of their asceticism (and necessarily attendant cant) and bigotry. Their neighbors in the middle states are composed of contributions from all countries of the civilized world, and have, as yet, no distinctive character; but it is probable that a very valuable one will be formed, in course of time, from such elements as the genial gaiety of the cavaliers, the patient industry of the Germans and Dutch, the vivacity of the French, the sobriety of the Scotch, the enterprise of the Irish, and the domestic tastes of the Swiss,--all of which, with their attendant drawbacks, go to compose the future American character. The chief pride of the New Englanders is in their unmixed descent;--a virtuous pride, but not the most favorable to a progression which must antiquate some of the qualities to which they are most attached. The European components of the other

127

population cherish some of the feudal prejudices and the territorial pride which they imported with them, and this is their peculiar drawback: but it appears that the enlarged liberality which they enjoy from being intermingled more than countervails the religious spirit of New England in opening the general heart and mind to the interests of the race at large. The progression of the middle states seems likely to be more rapid than that of New England, though the inhabitants of the northern states have hitherto taken and kept the lead.

It is the traveller's business to enter upon this course of observation wherever he goes. When he has ascertained the conditions under which the national character is forming,--whether its situation is insular or continental, colonial or independent, and whether it is descended from one race or more, he will proceed to observe the facts which indicate progress or the reverse.

*   *   *   *   *

The most obvious of these facts is the character of charity. Charity is everywhere. The human heart is always tender, always touched by visible suffering, under one form or another. The form which this charity takes is the great question.

In young and rude countries, an open-handed charity pervades the land. Everyone who comes in want to a dwelling has his immediate want relieved. The Arab gives from his mess to the hungerer who appears at the entrance of his tent. The negro brings rice and milk to the traveller who lies fainting under the palm. The poor are fed round convent-doors, morning and evening, where there are convents. In Ireland, it is a common practice to beg, in order to rise in the world,--a clear testimony to the practice of charity there. In all societies, the poor help the poorer; the depressed class aids the destitute. The existence of the charity may be considered a certainty. The inquiry is about its direction.

The lowest order of charity is that which is satisfied with relieving the immediate pressure of distress in individual cases. A higher is that which makes provision on a large scale for the relief of such distress; as when a nation passes on from common alms-giving to a general provision for the destitute. A higher still is when such provision is made in the way of anticipation, or for distant objects; as when the civilization of savages, the freeing of slaves, the treatment of the insane, or the education of the blind and deaf mutes is undertaken. The highest charity of all is that which aims at the prevention rather than the alleviation of evil. When any considerable number of a society are engaged in this work, the spirit of fraternity is busy there, and the progression of the society is ascertained. In such a community, it is allowed that though it is good to relieve the hungry, it is better to take care that all who work shall eat, as a matter of right: that though it is good to provide for the comfort and reformation of the guilty, it is better to obviate guilt: that though it is good to teach the ignorant who come in one's way, it is better to provide the means of knowledge, as of food, for all. In short, it is a nobler charity to prevent destitution, crime, and ignorance, than to relieve individuals who never ought to have been made destitute, criminal, and ignorant.

This war against the evils themselves, in preference to, but accompanied by, relief of the victims, has begun in many countries; and those which are the most busily occupied in the work must be considered the most advanced, and the most certain to advance. The observer must note the state of the work everywhere. In one country he will see the poor fed and clothed by charity, without any effort being made to relieve them from the pressure by which they are sunk in destitution. The spirit of brotherhood is not there; and such charity has nothing of the spirit of hope and progress in it. In another country, he will see the independent insisting on the right of the destitute to relief, and providing by law or custom for such relief. This is a great step, inasmuch as the interests of the helpless are taken up by the powerful,--a movement which must have something of the fraternal spirit for its impulse. In a third, he hears of prison discipline societies, missionary societies, temperance societies, and societies for the abolition of slavery. This is better still. It is looking wide,--so wide as that the spirit of charity acts as seeing the invisible,--the pagan trembling under the tabu, the negro outraged in his best affections, and the criminal hidden in the foul retreat of the common jail. It is also a training for looking deep; for these methods of charity all go to prevent the woes of future heathen generations, future slaves, drunkards, and criminals, as well as to soften the lot of those who exist. If, in a fourth society, the observer finds that the charity has gone deep as well as spread wide, and that the benevolent are tugging at the roots of indigence and crime, he may place this society above all the rest as to the brightness of its prospects. Such a movement can proceed only from the spirit of fraternity,--from the movers feeling it their own concern that any are depressed and endangered as they would themselves refuse to be. The elevation of the depressed classes in such a society, and the consequent progression of the whole, may be considered certain; for "sooner will the mother forget her sucking child" than the friends of their race forsake those for whom they have cared and labored with disinterested love and toil. Criminals will never be plunged back into their former state in America, nor women in France, nor negroes in the colonies of England. The spirit of justice (which is ultimately one with charity) has gone forth, not only conquering, but still to conquer.

To the prospects of the sufferers of society let the observer look; and he will discern the prospects of the society itself.

*   *   *   *   *

Useful arts and inventions spread so rapidly in these days of improving communication, that they are no longer the decisive marks of enlightenment in a people that they were when each nation had the benefit of its own discoveries, and little more. Yet it is worthy of remark what kinds of improvement are the most generally adopted; whether those which enhance the luxury of the rich, or such as benefit the whole society. It is worthy of remark whether the newest delight is in splendid club-houses, where gentlemen may command the rarest luxuries at a smaller expense than would have been possible without the aid of the principle of economy of association, or in the groups of mechanics' dwellings, where the same principle is applied in France to furnishing numbers with advantages of warmth, light, cookery, and cleanliness, which they could not otherwise have enjoyed. It is worth observing whether there are most mechanical inventions dedicated to the selfishness of the rich, or committed to the custom of the working classes. If the rich compose the great body of purchasers who are to be considered by inventors, the working classes are probably depressed. If there are most purchasers among the most numerous classes, the working order is rising, and the state of things is hopeful.--How speed the great discoveries and achievements which cannot, by any management, be confined to the few? How prospers the steam-engine, the rail-road,--strong hands which cannot be held back, by which a multitude of the comforts of life are extended to the poor, who could not reach up to them before? Do men glory most in the activity of these, or in the invention of a new pleasure for the satiated?

In the finer arts, for whom are heads and hands employed? The study of the ruins of all old countries tells the antiquary of the lives of the rich alone. There are churches which record the living piety or the dying penitence of the rich; priories and convents which speak of monkish idleness, and the gross luxuries which have cloaked themselves in asceticism; there are palaces of kings, castles of nobles, and villas of opulent commoners; but nowhere, except in countries recently desolated by war, are the relics of the abodes of the poor the study of the traveller. If he now finds skill bestowed on the buildings which are the exclusive resort of the laboring classes, and taste employed in their embellishment, it is clear that the order is rising. The record of each upward heave will remain for the observation of the future traveller, in the buildings to which they resort;--a record as indisputable as a mountain fissure presents to the geologist.

Time was when the dwellings of the opulent were ornamented with costly and beautiful works of art, while the eye of the peasant and the artisan found no other beauty to rest on than the face of his beloved, and the forms of his children. At this day, there are countries in Europe where the working man aspires to nothing more than to stick up an image of the Virgin, gay with colored paper, in a corner of his dwelling. But there are other lands where a higher taste for beauty is gratified. There are good prints provided cheap, to hang in the place of the ancient sampler or daub. Casts from all the finest works of the statuary, ancient and modern, are hawked about the streets, and may be seen in the windows where green parrots and brown cats in plaster used to annoy the eye. In societies where the working class is thus worked for, in the gratification of its finer tastes, the class must be rising. It is rising into the region of intellectual luxury, and must have been borne up thither by the expansion of the fraternal spirit.

*   *   *   *   *

The great means of progress, for individuals, for nations, and for the race at large, is the multiplication of Objects of interest. The indulgence of the passions is the characteristic of men and societies who have but one occupation and a single interest; while the passions cause comparatively little trouble where the intellect is active, and the life diversified with objects. Pride takes a safe direction, jealousy is diverted from its purposes of revenge, and anger combats with circumstances, instead of with human foes. The need of mutual aid, the habit of co-operation caused by interest in social objects, has a good effect upon men's feelings and manners towards each other; and out of this grows the mutual regard which naturally strengthens into the fraternal spirit. The Russian boor, imprisoned in his serfhood, cannot comprehend what it is to care for any but the few individuals who are before his eyes, and the Grand Lama has probably no great sympathy with the race; but in a town within whose compass almost all occupations are going forward, and where each feels more or less interest in what engages his neighbor, nothing of importance to the race can become known without producing more or less emotion. A famine in India, an earthquake in Syria, causes sorrow. The inhabitants meet to petition against the wrongs inflicted on people whom they have never seen, and give of the fruits of their labor to sufferers who have never heard of them, and from whom they can receive no return of acknowledgment. It is found that the more pursuits and aims are multiplied, the more does the appreciation of human happiness expand, till it becomes the interest which predominates over all the rest. This is an interest which works out its own gratification, more surely than any other. Wherever, therefore, the greatest variety of pursuits is met with, it is fair to conclude that the fraternal spirit of society is the most vigorous, and the society itself the most progressive.

This is as far as any nation has as yet attained,--to a warmer than common sympathy among its own members, and compassion for distant sufferers. When the time comes for nations to care for one another, and co-operate as individuals, such a people will be the first to hold out the right hand.

131

*   *   *   *   *

Manners have not been treated of separately from Morals in any of the preceding divisions of the objects of the traveller's observation. The reason is, that manners are inseparable from morals, or, at least, cease to have meaning when separated. Except as manifestations of morals, they have no interest, and can have no permanent existence. A traveller who should report of them exclusively is not only no philosopher, but does not merit the name of an observer; for he can have no insight into the matter which he professes to convey an account of. His interpretation of what is before his eyes is more likely to be wrong than correct, like that of the primitive star-gazers, who reported that the planets went backwards and forwards in the sky. To him, and to him only, who has studied the principles of morals, and thus possessed himself of a key to the mysteries of all social weal and woe, will manners be an index answering as faithfully to the internal movements, harmonious or discordant, of society, as the human countenance to the workings of the human heart.

Chapter 6: Discourse

He that questioneth much shall learn much, and content much;
but especially if he apply his questions to the skill of the
persons whom he asketh; for he shall give them occasion to
please themselves in speaking, and himself shall continually
gather knowledge.

Bacon

The Discourse of individuals is an indispensable commentary upon the classes of national facts which the traveller has observed. To begin the work of observation with registering this private discourse, is, as has been said, useless, from the diversity that there is in men's minds, and from the narrowness of the mental vision of each as he stands in a crowd. The testimony of no two would be found to agree; and, if the traveller depended upon them for his general facts, he could never furnish a record which could be trusted. But, the facts being once obtained by stronger evidence than individual testimony,--certain fixed points being provided round which testimony may gather,--the discourse of individuals assumes its proper value, and becomes illustrative where before it would have been only bewildering. The traveller must obtain all that he can of it. He must seek intercourse with all classes of the society he visits,--not only the rich and the poor, but those who may be classed by profession, pursuit, habits of mind, and turn of manners. He must converse with young men and maidens, old men and children, beggars and savans, postillions and potentates. He must study little ones at their mothers' knees, and flirtations in ball-rooms, and dealings in the market-place. He must overhear the mirth of revelers, and the grief of mourners. Wherever there is speech, he must devote himself to hear.

One way in which discourse serves as a commentary upon the things he has observed is in the exhibition of certain general characters of its own, which are accordant with the general facts he has registered. The conversation of almost every nation has its characteristics, like that of smaller societies.

133

The style of discourse in an English village is unlike that of a populous town; and the people of a town which is no thoroughfare talk differently from the inhabitants of one which is. In the same way is the general discourse of a whole people modified. In one country less regard is paid to truth in particulars, to circumstantial accuracy, than in another. One nation has more sincerity; another more kindliness in speech. One proses; another is light and sportive. One is frank; another reserved. One flatters the stranger; another is careless of him: and the discourse of the one is designed to produce a certain effect upon him; while that of the other flows out spontaneously, or is restrained, according to the traveller's own apparent humor. Such characteristics of the general discourse may be noted as a corroboration of suppositions drawn from other facts. They may be taken as evidence of the respective societies being catholic or puritanic in spirit; crude or accomplished; free and simple, or restrained and cautious; self-satisfied, or deficient in self-respect. The observer must be very careful not to generalize too hastily upon the discourse addressed to him; but there are everywhere large conclusions which he cannot help making. However wide the variety of individuals with whom he may converse, it is scarcely likely that he will meet in Spain with any number who will prose like the Americans; or in Germany with many who will treat him with the light jests of the French. Such general tendencies of any society as he may have been informed of by the study of things, he will find evidenced also by the general character of its discourse.

Another way in which discourse serves as a commentary, is by showing what interests the people most. If the observer goes with a free mind and an open heart, not full of notions and feelings of his own, but ready to resign himself to those of the people he visits,--if he commits himself to his sympathies, and makes himself one with those about him, he cannot but presently discover and appreciate what interests them most.

A high Tory in America will be more misled than enlightened by what is said to him, and so will a bigoted Republican in England. A prim Quaker will not understand the French from half a year of Parisian conversation, any more than a mere dandy would feel at home at Jena or Heidelberg. But a traveller free from gross prejudice and selfishness can hardly be many days in a new society without learning what are its chief interests. Even savages would speak to him of the figure-head of their canoe; and others would go through, in time, each its own range of topics, till the German had poured out to him his philosophical views, and the Frenchman his solicitudes for the amelioration of society, and the American his patriotic aspirations, and the Swiss his domestic sentiment. Whatever may be the restrictions imposed by rulers upon discourse, whatever may be the penalties imposed upon particular kinds of communication, all are unavailing in the presence of sympathy. At its touch the abundance of the heart will gush out at the lips. Men are so made that they cannot but speak of what interests them most to those who most share the interest. This is a decree of nature by which the decrees of despots are annulled. The power of a ruler may avail to keep an observer on his own side the frontier; but, if he has once passed it, it is his own fault if he does not become as well acquainted with the prevailing sentiment of the inhabitants, amidst the deadest public silence, as if it were shouted out to the four winds. If he carries a simple mind and an open heart, there is no mine in Siberia so deep but the voice of complaint will come up to him from it, and no home so watched by priests but that he will know what is concealed from the confessor. All this would do little more than mislead him by means of his sympathies, if such confidence were his only means of knowledge; but, coming in corroboration of what he has learned in the large elsewhere, it becomes unquestionable evidence of what it is that interests the people most.

He must bear in mind that there are a few universal interests which everywhere stand first, and that it is the modification of these by local influences which he has to observe; and also what comes next in order to these. For instance, the domestic are the primary interests among all human beings. It is so where the New England father dismisses his sons to the West,--and where the Hindoo mother deserts her infants to seek the shade of her husband through the fire,--and where the Spanish parent consigns her youngest to the convent,--as truly as where the Norwegian peasant enlarges his roof to admit another and another family of his descendants. It is for the traveller to trust the words and tones of parental love which meet his ear in every home of every land; and to mark by what it is that this prime and universal interest is modified, so as to produce such sacrifice of itself. Taking the affection for granted, which the private discourse of parents and children compels him to do, what light does he find cast upon the influence of the priests here, and pride of territory there;--upon the superstition which is the weakness of one people, and the social ambition in the midst of poverty which is the curse of another!

He must also find out from the conversation of the people he visits what is their particular interest, from observing what ranks next to those which are universal. In one country, parents love their families first, and wealth next; in another, their families first, and glory next; in a third, their families first, and liberty next; and so on, through the whole range of objects of human desire. Once having discerned the mode, he will find it easy to take the suffrage without much danger of mistake.

The chief reason why the discourse of individuals, apart from the observation of classes of facts, is almost purely deceptive as to morals, is that the traveller can see no more than one in fifty thousand of the people, and has no security that those he meets are a sample of the whole. This difficulty does not interfere with one very important advantage which he may obtain from conversation,--knowledge of and light upon particular questions. A stranger might wish to learn the state of Christianity in England. If he came to London, and began with conversation, he might meet a Church-of-England-man one day, a Catholic the next, a Presbyterian the third, a Quaker the fourth, a Methodist the fifth, and so on, till the result was pure bewilderment. But if he conversed with intelligent persons, he would find that questions were pending respecting the church and dissent,--involving the very principles of the administration of religion. The opinions he hears upon these questions may be as various as the persons he converses with. He may be unable to learn the true characters of the statesmen and religious leaders concerned in their management: but he gains something of more value. Light is thrown upon the state of things from which alone these questions could have arisen. From free newspapers he might have learned the nature of the controversy; but in social intercourse much more is presented to him. He sees the array of opinions marshaled on each side, or on all the sides of the question; and receives an infinite number of suggestions and illustrations which could never have reached him but from the conflict of intellects, and the diversity of views and statements with which he is entertained in discourse. The traveller in every country should thus welcome the discussion of questions in which the inhabitants are interested, taking strenuous care to hear the statements of every party. From the intimate connection of certain modes of opinion with all great questions, he will gain light upon the whole condition of opinion from its exhibition in one case. New subjects of research will be brought within his reach; new paths of inquiry will be opened; new trains of ideas will be awakened, and fresh minds brought into communication with his own. If he can secure the good fortune of conversing with the leaders on both sides of great questions,--with the men who have made it a pursuit to collect all the facts of the case, and to follow out its principles,--there is no estimating his advantage. There is, perhaps, scarcely one great subject of national controversy which, thus opened to him, would not afford him glimpses into all the other general affairs of the day; and each time that his mind grasps a definite opposition of popular opinion, he has accomplished a stage in his pilgrimage of inquiry into the tendencies of a national mind. He will therefore be anxious to engage all he meets in full and free conversation on prevailing topics, leaving it to them to open their minds in their own way, and only taking care of his own,--that he preserves his impartiality, and does no injustice to question or persons by bias of his own.

In arranging his plans for conversing with all kinds of people, the observer will not omit to cultivate especially the acquaintance of persons who themselves see the most of society. The value of their testimony on particular points must depend much on that of their minds and characters; but, from the very fact of their having transactions with a large portion of society, they cannot avoid affording many lights to a stranger which he could obtain by no other means. The conversation of lawyers in a free country, of physicians, of merchants and manufacturers in central trading situations, of innkeepers and of barbers everywhere, must yield him much which he could not have collected for himself. The minds of a great variety of people are daily acting upon the thoughts of such, and the facts of a great variety of lives upon their experience; and whether they be more or less wise in the use of their opportunities, they must be unlike what they would have been in a state of seclusion. If the stranger listens to what they are most willing to tell, he may learn much of popular modes of thinking and feeling, of modes of living, acting, and transacting, which will confirm and illustrate impressions and ideas which he had previously gained from other sources.

The result of the whole of what he hears will probably be to the traveller of the same kind with that which the journey of life yields to the wisest of its pilgrims. As he proceeds, he will learn to condemn less, and to admire, not less, but differently. He will find no intellect infallible, no judgment free from prejudice, and therefore no affections without their bias; but, on the other hand, he will find no error which does not branch out of some truth; no wrath which has not some reason in it; nothing wrong which is not the perversion of something right; no wickedness that is not weakness. If he is compelled to give up the adoration of individuals, the man-worship which is the religion of young days, he surrenders with it the spirit of contempt which ought also to be proper to youth. To a healthy mind it is impossible to mix largely with men, under a variety of circumstances, and wholly to despise either societies or individuals; so magnificent is the intellect of men in combination, so universal are their most privately nourished affections. He must deny himself the repose of implicit faith in the intellect of any one; but he cannot refuse the luxury of trust in the moral power of the whole. Instead of the complete set of dogmas with which he was perhaps once furnished, on the authority of a few individuals, he brings home a store of learning on the great subject of human prejudices: but he cannot have watched the vast effects of a community of sentiment,--he cannot have observed multitudes tranquillized into social order, stimulated to social duty, and even impelled to philanthropic self-sacrifice, without being convinced that men were made to live in a bond of brotherhood. He cannot have sat in conversation under the village elm, or in sunny vineyards, or by the embers of the midnight fire, without knowing how spirit is formed to unfold itself to spirit; and how, when the solitary is set in families, his sympathies bind him to them by such a chain as selfish interest never yet wove. He cannot have travelled wisely and well without being convinced that moral power is the force which lifts man to be not only lord of the earth, but scarcely below the angels; and that the higher species of moral power, which are likely to come more and more into use, clothe him in a kind of divinity to which angels themselves might bow.--No one will doubt this who has been admitted into that range of sanctuaries, the homes of nations; and who has witnessed the godlike achievements of the servants, sages, and martyrs, who have existed wherever man has been.

Part Three: Mechanical Methods

In sea-voyages, where there is nothing to be seen but sky and
sea, men make diaries; but in land-travel, wherein so much is to
be observed, they omit it.

--Bacon

Stick to your journal course; the breach of custom
Is breach of all.

--Cymbeline

Travellers cannot be always on the alert, any more than other men. Their
hours of weariness and of capricious idleness come, as at home; and there is
no security against their occurring at inconvenient times,--just when some
characteristic spectacle is to be witnessed, or some long-desired information is
in waiting. By a little forethought, the observer may guard against some of the
effects of seizures of apathy. If he would rather sleep in the carriage than get
out to see a waterfall, he can only feel ashamed, and rouse himself to do his
duty: but, by precaution, he may guard himself from passing by some things
less beautiful than waterfalls, and to have seen which is less necessary to his
reputation as a traveller; but which yet he will be more sorry eventually to
have lost.

To keep himself up to his business, and stimulate his flagging attention, he
should provide himself, before setting out, with a set of queries, so prepared
as to include every great class of facts connected with the condition of a
people, and so divided and arranged as that he can turn to the right set at the
fitting moment.--These queries are not designed to be thrust into the hand of
any one who may have information to give. They should not even be allowed
to catch his eye. The traveller who has the air of taking notes in the midst of
conversation, is in danger of bringing away information imperfect as far as it
goes, and much restricted in quantity in comparison with what it would be if

he allowed it to be forgotten that he was a foreigner seeking information. If he permits the conversation to flow on naturally, without checking it by the production of the pencil and tablets, he will, even if his memory be not of the best, have more to set down at night than if he noted on the spot, as evidence, what a companion might be saying to him. But a glance in the morning at his list of queries may suggest inquiries which he might not otherwise remember to make; and they will help him afterwards to arrange the knowledge he has gained. He can be constantly adding to them as he goes along, and as new subjects arise, till he is in possession of a catechism on the facts which indicate morals and manners; which must prevent his researches being so capricious, and his information so vague as his moods and his idleness would otherwise occasionally make them.

The character of these queries must, of course, depend much on where the traveller means to go. A set which would suit one nation would not completely apply to any other. The observer will do wisely to employ his utmost skill in framing them. His cares will be better bestowed on this than even on his travelling appointments, important as these are to his comfort. When he has done his best in the preparation of his lists, he must still keep on the watch to enlarge them, as occasion arises.

Some travellers unite in one the functions of the query list and the journal: having the diary headed and arranged for the reception of classified information. But this seems to be debasing the function of a journal, whose object ought to be to reflect the mind of a traveller, and give back to him hereafter the image of what he thought and felt day by day. This is its primary function;--a most useful one, as every traveller knows who has kept one during a year's wandering in a foreign country. On his return, he laughs at the crudity of the information, and the childishness of the impressions, set down in the opening pages; and traces, with as much wonder as interest, the gradual expansion of his knowledge, education of his perceptions, and maturing of his judgments as to what is before him, as week succeeds to week, and each month mellows the experience of the last.

The subordinate purpose of the journal is to record facts; and the way in which this is done ought not to depend on the stationer's rule, but on the nature of the traveller's mind. No man can write down daily all that he learns in a day's travel. It ought to be a matter of serious consideration with him what he will insert, and what trust to his memory. The simplest method seems to be to set down what is most likely to be let slip, and to trust to the memory what the affections and tastes of the traveller will not allow him to forget. One who especially enjoys intimate domestic intercourse will write, not fireside conversations, but the opinions of statesmen, and the doctrine of parties on great social questions. One whose tastes are religious will note less on the subject of public worship and private religious discourse, than dates, numbers, and facts on subjects of subordinate interest. All should record anecdotes and sayings which illustrate character. These are disjointed, and will escape almost any memory, if not secured in writing. Those who do not draw should also note scenery. A very few descriptive touches will bring back a landscape, with all its human interest, after a lapse of years: while perhaps there is no memory in the world which will present unaided the distinctive character of a succession of scenes. The returned traveller is ashamed to see the extent of his record of his personal feelings. His changes of mood, his sufferings from heat or cold, from hunger or weariness, are the most interesting things to him at the moment; and down they go, in the place of things much better worth recording, and he pays the penalty in many a blush hereafter. His best method will be to record as little as possible about himself; and, of other things, most of what he is pretty sure to forget, and least of what he can hardly help remembering.

Generally speaking, he will find it desirable to defer the work of generalization till he gets home. In the earlier stages of his journey, at least, he will restrict his pen to the record of facts and impressions; or, if his mind should have an unconquerable theorizing tendency, he will be so far cautious as to put down his inferences conjecturally. It is easy to do this; and it may make an eternal difference to the observer's love of truth, and attainment of it, whether he preserves his philosophic thoughts in the form of dogmas or of queries.

Though it is commonly spoken of as a settled thing that the journal should be written at night, there are many who do not agree to this. There are some whose memory fails when the body is tired, and who find themselves clear-headed about many things in the morning which were but imperfectly remembered before they had the refreshment of sleep. The early morning is probably the best time for the greater number; but it is a safe general rule that the journal should be written in the interval when the task is pleasantest. Whether the regularity be pleasant or not, (and to the most conscientious travellers it is the most agreeable,) the entries ought to be made daily, if possible. The loss incurred by delay is manifest to anyone who has tried. The shortest entries are always those which have been deferred. The delay of a single day is found to reduce the matter unaccountably. In the midst of his weariness and unwillingness to take out his pen, the traveller may comfort himself by remembering that he will reap the reward of diligence in satisfaction when he gets home. He may assure himself that no lines that he can write can ever be more valuable than those in which he hives his treasures of travel. If he turns away from the task, he will have uneasy feelings connected with his journey as often as he looks back upon it;--feelings of remorse for his idleness, and of regret for irretrievable loss. If, on the other hand, he perseveres in the daily duty, he will go forward each morning with a disburthened mind, and will find, in future years, that he loves the very blots and weather-stains on the pages which are so many remembrancers of his satisfactory labors and profitable pleasures.

Besides the journal, the traveller should have a note-book,--always at hand,--not to be pulled out before people's eyes, for the entry of facts related, but to be used for securing the transient appearances which, though revealing so much to an observing mind, cannot be recalled with entire precision. In all the countries of the world, groups by the wayside are the most eloquent of pictures. The traveller who lets himself be whirled past them, unobservant or unrecording, loses more than any devices of inquiry at his inn can repair. If he can sketch, he should rarely allow a characteristic group of persons, or nook of scenery, to escape his pencil. If he cannot use the pencil, a few written words will do. Two lines may preserve for him an exemplification which may be of great future value.--The farmers' wives of New England, talking over the snake-fence at sunset, are in themselves an illustration of many things: so is the stern Indian in his blanket-cloak, standing on a mound on the prairie; so is the chamois hunter on his pinnacle, and the pedestrian student in the valleys of the Hartz, and the pine-cutters on the steeps of Norway, and the travelling merchant on the dyke in Holland, and the vine-dressers in Alsace, and the beggars in the streets of Spanish cities, and all the children of all countries at their play. The traveller does not dream of passing unnoticed the cross in the wilderness, beneath which some brother pilgrim lies murdered; or the group of brigands seen in the shadow of the wood; or a company of Sisters of Charity, going forth to their deeds of mercy; or a pair of inquisitors, busy on the errands of the Holy Office; or anything else which strongly appeals to his imagination or his personal feelings. These pictures, thus engraved in his memory, he may safely leave to be entered in his journal, night or morning: but groups and scenes which ought to be quite as interesting, because they reveal the thoughts and ways of men, (the more familiarly the more faithfully,) should be as earnestly observed; and, to give them a chance of equal preservation, they should be noted on the instant. If a foreigner opens his eyes after a nap in travelling an Irish road, would it not be wise to note at once what he sees that he could not see elsewhere? He perceives that the green lanes which branch off from the road are more crowded with foliage, and less definite in their windings, than any other green lanes he has seen near high roads. The road itself is sui generis, with its border of rank grass, with tufts of straggling briers, and its rough stone walls, fringed with weeds, and gay with wild flowers. A beggarly wretch is astride on the top, singing the Doxology to the tune of Paudeen O'Rafferty, and keeping time with his heels:

and, some way off, an old man crouches in the grass, playing cards,--the right hand against the left,--reviling the winner, and tenderly consoling the loser. Presently the stranger passes a roofless hut, where he sees, either a party of boys and girls throwing turf for a handful of meal, or a beggar-woman and her children resting in the shade of the walls to eat their cold potatoes. Such scenes could be beheld nowhere but in Ireland: but there is no country in the world where groups and pictures as characteristic do not present themselves to the observing eye, and in such quick succession that they are liable to be confused and lost, if not secured at the moment by brief touches of pencil or pen. The note-book should be the repository of such.

Mechanical methods are nothing but in proportion to the power which uses them; as the intellectual accomplishments of the traveller avail him little, and may even bring him back less wise than he went out,--a wanderer from truth, as well as from home,--unless he sees by a light from his heart shining through the eyes of his mind. He may see, and hear, and record, and infer, and conclude forever; and he will still not understand if his heart be idle,--if he have not sympathy. Sympathy by itself may do much: with fit intellectual and mechanical aids, it cannot but make the traveller a wise man. His journey may be but for a brief year, or even month; but if, by his own sympathy, he grasps and brings home to himself the life of a fresh portion of his race, he gains a wisdom for which he will be the better forever.

Footnotes

[A] Penny Magazine, vol. ii. p. 309.

[B] Volney's Survey of the Revolutions of Empires, pp. 25, 26.

[C] Mme. D'Aunoy.

[D] Adam Smith, "Wealth of Nations."

[E] Jacob, "Travels in the South of Spain."

[F] HOME, by Miss Sedgwick, pp. 37, 39.

[G] An exception to this may meet the eye of a traveller once in a lifetime. There is a village church-yard in England where the following inscription is to be seen. After the name and date occurs the following:

> He was a Bad Son,
> A Bad Husband,
> A Bad Father.

"The wicked shall be turned into Hell."

[H] Edinburgh Review, vol. xxxix. p. 67.

[I] Edinburgh Review, vol. xlvi. p. 309.

[J] Edinburgh Review, vol. xxvi. pp. 7, 8.

[K] Corn Law Rhymer. Elliott of Sheffield.

[L] Travels of Minna and Godfrey in Many Lands, p. 53.

[M] Rogers's Italy, p. 172.

[N] Memoirs of an American Lady.

THE END

Made in the USA
Lexington, KY
29 December 2016